Praise for *Rethinking Work*

"Will increase your 'bump rate'—your ability to ~~understand~~ t you need,
meet new people, and giv

—**Robert M. Krim, PhD, ex**
Boston History & Innov

"Embraces all of life. A blue ~~print for building relationships~~ as our relationship to work, it offers a path for discovering where and how you will make
a difference personally and professionally."

—**Lenore Mewton, MSW, PCC, host, CoachInc., Coach University Career SIG**

"Captures the essence of finding purposeful work and balance in a society that
has become unbalanced. It is more important than ever to read Rethinking
Work and seriously consider the message to reach inside of yourself to create
your future."

—**Thomas Bendheim, president and CEO, The Colibri Group**

"Hakim is right on the mark with his insights into the impact of globalization
and the importance of seeking meaningful work. The message is essential for
finding success in the new economy."

—**Peter McAteer, director and CLO, United Nations Development Programme**

"With the wisdom and clarity of someone who has coached and mentored hundreds of people, Hakim speaks from the heart and leads by example. To borrow
a famous tag line, it's not enough to 'just do it'. Dig deep and do it now, with
your unique passion."

—**Dwight Griesman, VP & practice leader, Forrester Research**

"Hakim reminds us that the only career compass is deep inside, perhaps hidden
under many layers of fear and obligation. Here's help for tossing those aside
and reigniting your passion for work."

—**Maureen Anderson, host of the syndicated radio program *The Career Clinic***

"*Rethinking Work is for people who expect a lot from life and from themselves. Hakim calls us to become wise and thereby to experience the benefits of a life well lived and work well done.*"

—Mary H. Jacobsen, author of *Hand-Me-Down Dreams*

"*Shows us how to release renewed energy and creativity to explore the spectrum of our personal and professional passions.*"

—Richard MacMillan, VP for Institutional Advancement, Massachusetts College of Art

"*Raises the right questions, provides a compass to find the answers within, and, through numerous examples, shifts the balance of power from the fears that keep us stuck to the confidence that moves us forward.*"

—Herb Shumway, SVP Finance and Operations, CFO, NMS Communications

"*Like a Sunday drive, relaxes you enough to explore, examine your feelings and attitudes toward work, and imagine other possibilities. It's an easy read that will support you, even if you choose to go off on your own.*"

—Ted Selker, associate professor, MIT Media Lab; director, Industrial Design Intelligence

"*Priceless—filled with provoking ideas, encouraging case studies, practical exercises, and insightful questions that will change your life.*"

—Mark J. Campbell, author of *Five Gifts of Insightful Leaders*

"*A fantastic collection of personal and practical lessons on how to effectively take charge of your life and find personally and professionally rewarding work that makes a difference.*"

—Thomas Kristoph, director, Development & Retention, Dynamics Research Corporation

"*A wonderfully practical book for all who want to explore new options and change career directions. Full of useful tips and great examples that can help you take charge of your career and move forward.*"

—Betsy Collard, director, Alumni Volunteer Relations and Career Services, Stanford Alumni Association

rethinking Work

rethinking
Work

Are You Ready to Take Charge?

Cliff Hakim

Davies-Black Publishing
Mountain View, California

Published by Davies-Black Publishing, a division of CPP, Inc., 1055 Joaquin Road, 2nd Floor, Mountain View, CA 94043; 800-624-1765.

Special discounts on bulk quantities of Davies-Black books are available to corporations, professional associations, and other organizations. For details, contact the Director of Marketing and Sales at Davies-Black Publishing: 650-691-9123; fax 650-623-9271.

Copyright 2007 by Cliff Hakim. All rights reserved. No portion of this book may be reproduced, stored in a retrieval system, or transmitted in any form or media or by any means, electronic, mechanical, photocopying, recording, or otherwise, without the prior written permission of the publisher, except in the case of brief quotations embodied in critical articles or reviews.

Davies-Black and its colophon are registered trademarks of CPP, Inc.

Visit the Davies-Black Publishing Web site at www.daviesblack.com.

Cover illustration: Larry Corby

Printed in the United States of America.
11 10 09 08 07 10 9 8 7 6 5 4 3 2 1

Library of Congress Cataloging-in-Publication Data
Hakim, Cliff
    Rethinking work : are you ready to take charge? / Cliff Hakim. — 1st ed.
        p. cm.
    Includes index.
    ISBN: 978-0-89106-230-1 (pbk.)
    1. Work—Psychological aspects. 2. Lifespan, Productive. I. Title.
    HF5548.8.H225 2007
    650.1—dc22

                                                              2007012859

FIRST EDITION
First printing 2007

To my clients—for their spark, inspiration, and courage as they challenge themselves and life to become and contribute who they are

CONTENTS

PREFACE

"I'm at a crossroads. How do I sort out my next move?" This statement is the one most frequently raised by my clients as they initiate the process of rethinking their work. They are really asking, Who do I want to become? What do I truly want to do with my precious time? How do I become better at my job, prouder of my career, and more of a contributor to this planet?

Pushed by outside forces—debts, tuition costs, rent and mortgage payments, everyday expenses, and others' wishes and demands—they all nonetheless feel pulled by an inner voice that says, Time is passing, and I'd like my work—my life—to count toward something more than just a paycheck. One client said, "I want less stress—which is caused by sitting at my desk most days thinking about how disappointed I am in my career—and more success—which I define as rewarding work for which I earn enough money but use more of my intellect and passion as I interact with customers in an energized work environment."

The purpose of *Rethinking Work* is to promote this profound shift from "outer economy" control to "inner economy" self-leadership—by putting you in charge of your job and career at a time when you, your company, and the marketplace are changing. As a career consultant and strategist, it's my job to help people find places to stand in an ever-changing economic climate while doing work that allows them to remain true to themselves. My hope is that this book will do the same for you.

The guidelines I put forward represent the culmination of more than twenty years of experience shepherding men and women through major work and life transitions. Whether you're just entering the workforce or changing jobs for the umpteenth time, whether you're working for a company or are in business for yourself, this book will show you how to take charge of your future and stop feeling like the victim of sudden economic shifts. In short, it will show you how to make your job give back to you.

Rethinking Work is designed to help you ask questions, generate options, and discover answers in the most efficient and timely way—taking the very real demands of economics into account. As my client Mark said, "Searching for a new direction isn't easy. If I don't hurry up and get clear, how will I pay my mortgage?"

I recognize—and don't discount—the very real pressure to earn a living and honor your financial responsibilities. But, I want to show you how to find a more satisfying way to do so. Chapter 1 introduces the Rethinking Work® process, which consists of three steps that help you do just that. Then, the three steps are explained in Chapter 2, "The Right to Reflect," Chapter 3, "The Permission to Explore," and Chapter 4, "The Courage to Engage." The three active verbs—*reflect, explore,* and *engage*—are key and can become inner commands to yourself.

Throughout this book, inspiring success stories and practical exercises will engage your spirit and help you redefine your relationship to work. Note that *Rethinking Work* does not portray a fad or fashion. Rather, it offers a set of beliefs and tools that can help you create your future again and again. My hope is that, by reading this book, you will validate the values that are essential for your well-being and then turn your job around so that it works for you.

—*Cliff Hakim*

ACKNOWLEDGMENTS

This book is a compilation of collective wisdom, spirit, effort, and dreams. As I wrote, I imagined all the people who had contributed to it, directly or indirectly, holding hands, and realized that they would easily encompass an entire city block. As I was engaged in rethinking work—managing my independence, reflecting on and exploring my experience and thoughts, and engaging my interdependence—I was rarely writing alone!

Rethinking Work opens with the dedication, "To my clients—for their spark, inspiration, and courage as they challenge themselves and life to become and contribute who they are." In my experience, it is never easy to do the work of understanding and believing in oneself and acting on what matters so that life becomes, at every stage, personally fulfilling and a gift to others. Every client's story required numerous acts of courage—vulnerability and bravery—for that individual to honestly face him- or herself and find his or her niche in the world. My clients have been the seeds of this book and their successes the harvest. I thank them for contributing to my spirit and touching and inspiring so many others with their example.

Each of the following was a core contributor to the birth of *Rethinking Work*.

- Valerie Andrews, my writing muse: I thank her for her hope—her willingness to believe in things not yet achieved—and for her wisdom and guidance.

- John Willig, my agent and friend: I thank him for our years of philosophical and inspirational discussions, reminding me that "all it takes is one to love you" (and, in fact, Davies-Black Publishing did).

- Amy Fardella, my wife and best friend: I thank her for believing in her heart that if anyone can "rethink work," I could, even when my path was most serpentine and foggy.

- Gabriella Hakim, my daughter: I thank her for her curiosity—questions—and pride in her dad, "the author."

- Nora Hakim, my mother: I am grateful for her love, her respect for the power of the written word, and her joy at seeing mine in print.

The Davies-Black team has been an exemplary partner of the Rethinking Work kind, beginning with Connie Kallback, Senior Acquisitions Editor, saying about my manuscript, "What's not to love?" I thank Connie for making every effort to preserve and express the Rethinking Work spirit—its stories, tools, questions, and dialogue that give the reader opportunities to listen to and learn from others and then listen to their inner voice, choose their own path, and stretch into the wider world.

When I saw the Rethinking Work cover design for the first time, I let out a big whoop! Laura Simonds, Director of Marketing and Sales, had listened to my ideas and passed them on to Laura Ackerman-Shaw, Divisional Director of Publishing Services. Both Lauras intuitively understood that the "flying ace," a creation of illustrator Larry Corby (a genius with a funny bone and a big heart), along with the bold use of red and black, would uniquely express the clear and fresh professional value of this book. Thank you to book designers Mark Reis and Brad Boettcher of Percolator Graphic Design for pulling all the elements together into a cover that grabs readers' attention and that expresses my wish for them: that they soar, again and again, in their work life.

Acknowledging the team that created the cover would be incomplete without honoring Elles Gianocostas, my Web site designer. Elles's careful choice of font and overall design reflected my brand and inspired the cover.

To thrive, ideas must be carefully produced. My appreciation goes to Jill Anderson-Wilson, Managing Editor at Davies-Black, a shepherd alchemist, who safeguarded the book's integrity and clarity while keeping the production schedule rolling to meet our publication date. I also thank production artist Francie Curtiss for her meticulous work in turning the edited manuscript into a book and seeing the process through to completion.

Rebecca Weisman, Manager of Marketing and Sales, thank you for your partnering efforts with Laura Simonds to launch *Rethinking Work* and see it take off in a crowded, competitive, and hungry marketplace.

Thank you—the reader—too, for contemplating the ideas in *Rethinking Work* and trusting them enough to risk taking new steps in your journey to untold destinations.

ARE YOU READY TO TAKE CHARGE?

People engage in the career consulting process only when they are ready. For many, recognizing that state of readiness can be a real challenge. Fear, busy schedules, and impatience can thwart people's insight into their needs and derail even the best intentions to start a development program. I've heard clients say, for example, "I don't know what happened. In the past three or four years my company has changed, but I haven't!"

Following is a Readiness Guide that has emerged from my career consulting practice. You can use it to assess, measure, and affirm your readiness. If you check three or more of the items, you are likely ready to start the Rethinking Work process.

RETHINKING WORK®
READINESS GUIDE

Do you want to . . .

☐ make more worthwhile contributions?

☐ take charge of your attitude?

☐ reawaken your spirit?

☐ fully express your passion?

☐ overcome your work fears?

☐ stay in your current job and grow there?

☐ take control of your work life?

☐ better align with customers' needs?

☐ maintain a clear sense of self while you work with others?

☐ establish a new work attitude?

☐ set a leadership example?

☐ approach work with grace?

☐ inspire others?

YOUR CORE QUESTIONS

OPENING YOUR PERSPECTIVES

Life isn't about finding yourself. Life is about creating yourself.
GEORGE BERNARD SHAW

Many of us are so caught up in the financial rat race that we feel we can't afford to think about personally rewarding work. An underlying sense of anxiety and panic wells up as we confront the future—since we are now hopping from job to job faster than ever before. In fact, most of us are likely to pursue two or three careers within our lifetime. According to the U.S. Department of Labor, the average 35-year-old has already changed jobs nine times or more. There's no telling which sector will suffer next from downsizing or belt-tightening, consequently requiring us to retrain and regroup.

At the same time, our hiring has been shifting overseas—in the past three years, the number of jobs outsourced to foreign countries has tripled—so the competition for U.S. jobs is often fierce. Never has the message been so clear: To survive, we need to step outside the box and reinvent our relationship to work. A pink slip can strike terror into the hearts of the most capable professionals, and many people are biding their time—just holding on—in jobs that have become routine and boring. Yet, when I look at our current situation, I see more than a crisis: I see a host of opportunities.

UNDERSTANDING THE CHANGING WORK ENVIRONMENT

The people who make up Generation X, born between 1965 and 1979, joined the workforce with a different mind-set than did their elders. They landed in a global environment characterized by fever-ish competition, severed loyalty bonds, and rampant unpredictabil-ity. Since the 1980s, more than 30 million workers have been laid off, downsized, and rightsized. Employees have learned to innovate or perish. In other words, staying afloat requires them to take their cre-ativity—and flexibility—to work.

Gen Xers are savvy about today's social challenges: how to pre-serve the environment, do business in an ethical way, and create products and institutions that will help build a better world. They see work as a continual learning laboratory. They assume they will make many different contributions throughout their lifetime and, in the process, they will perfect the art of reinventing both their work and their ideals.

When the Baby Boomers were broadsided by unprecedented changes in the workplace, they struggled but didn't fold. Perhaps the most prominent trait of the 78 million Americans born between

1946 and 1964 is their refusal to give up their dreams when faced with a volatile economy. Much can be learned from the resilience of these individuals.

Jack, a 58-year-old manager, has no intention of retiring anytime soon. "I need to make a contribution to this planet first, and I want to figure out what that contribution will be," he says. At 50, Valerie, an accountant, says, "I've been working in a profession that has little heart. Passion will feed my next career move." Pilar, a 43-year-old entrepreneur, wants to answer the question, How much money do I really need to feel secure and do creative work? "My answer will help me take back my time," she says, "and do the kind of work that challenges me to grow personally as well as give to others."

Bill Gates of Microsoft Corporation and Steve Jobs of Apple Inc. serve as inspirational models. They have rechanneled their strengths and expanded their vision over the past two decades, giving us technologies that have contributed to the economy and driven global change. Although they have certainly achieved both wealth and recognition, I suspect they will keep pursuing their individual dreams, leaving us a legacy of social innovation at the same time.

The Baby Boomers, once told to grow up, have apparently decided to grow up but not old. For example, at the 2006 Super Bowl, the sixtyish Rolling Stones were more than just rolling—they were rocking. Other famous Boomers—from Oprah Winfrey to Bill Clinton to Steven Spielberg—continue to raise the bar for everyone, showing that it's possible to make new contributions at every stage of life.

The days when we worked for one or two companies and then gracefully retired are clearly over. Both Baby Boomers and Gen Xers are involved in a constant process of reinvention. A new three Rs— repositioning, retraining, and regrouping—now characterize the rules for everyone who works.

DISCOVERING YOUR INNER ECONOMY

Our attitudes toward money are changing as well. We're beginning to look less at the *outer economy,* which is driven by market forces, and more at the *inner economy,* which refers to how and why we drive ourselves. The core of my work for the past twenty years has been to help people recognize their inner economy—the values that are essential to their well-being. During this process, I've shown men and women how to bounce back after downsizing, find jobs that are better suited to their skills and interests, and even strike out on their own as consultants and entrepreneurs.

I've been called a Boomer poster boy because I was born in 1951 and from an early age had a desire to blaze my own path, inspire others, and squeeze every drop of passion from life. My dreams haven't changed, but the broad financial picture certainly has. In 1974, I bought a used Volkswagen Bug for $600, filled the tank for less than $2.50, and drove from Boston to San Francisco by way of the Nevada and Wyoming deserts and the Rocky Mountains. When I returned to Boston two years later, I sold the car, only slightly worn, for the same price. In my first job as a teacher, I earned less than $13,000 a year and still managed to save a part of my paycheck. Today, I earn multiples of that amount, yet I am increasingly challenged to add to my financial reserves. Insurance fees, mortgage payments, tuition costs, home maintenance expenses, grocery bills, and so on loom large, fighting for and gobbling up almost everything I earn. No matter what our earning power is, we're all caught up in the same spiral of spending—both longing for and driving for more—and inflation. In 1974, the U.S. national debt was less than $1 trillion. Today, it has surpassed $8 trillion.

The way to achieve peace of mind in the midst of all this chaos is this: Don't link your worth and happiness to an infinitely hiccupping economic cycle. You'll only thrash around and then end up exhausted and in debt. Don't rely on the conventional wisdom that newer or bigger automatically equals better either. Someone will always be knocking on your door with a new idea requiring you to dip deeper into your pockets. You need to become your own sage, determining how to engage the outer economy and nourish your inner economy by holding on to your values and your sense of self-worth.

FINDING YOUR PLACE

The outer economy undeniably governs the costs of food, housing, schooling, health care, and transportation, as well as the amount of time we have to pursue our dreams. Not only do we have limited control over this economy, but we are also constantly bombarded—and frequently seduced—by its messages: Buy more, wear what's fashionable, drive the newest car, follow the latest trends, expect instant success. Within a single generation, our ideas about stability and security have changed, and we're caught in a rapidly shrinking universe where workers are hired and then summarily dismissed. Whether you do a good job or a bad job matters less than before. In this economic climate, you *will* lose your job, and you will have to redefine yourself more times than you ever imagined.

Add to all this the probability that you'll live longer than your predecessors, and you can see how important it is to take your dreams—and your creativity—seriously. Given ongoing advances in medical science, the human life span may soon reach 100. The midpoint age will then be a healthy 50 or 60 years. Will we be able to save enough retirement money to tide us over for forty or so years? Will we even *want* to retire, or will we become bored and seek a new life purpose in a new kind of work? We Boomers have already rebelled against life's predictable, linear path. Every indication suggests that we will continue to reshape our lives by challenging ourselves in our 60s and beyond.

The AARP Global Aging Program International Retirement Security Survey report in July 2005 showed that 40 percent of global respondents intend to work in one form or another after they officially retire. Nearly 70 percent of U.S. respondents are interested in working during retirement. Shaping a better, longer life will require a good deal of persistence and physical and mental fitness and flexibility.

To find your place—to take charge of your job and career—you'll need to ask yourself, Am I able to move past the victim-of-statistics mentality? How can I create a spot for myself in a youth-oriented culture? If the climb to the top is over, how do I enjoy, earn, and contribute from where I am right now?

RECOGNIZING THAT WE ARE ALL SELF-EMPLOYED

In my book *We Are All Self-Employed: How to Take Control of Your Career* (2nd ed., Berrett-Koehler, 2003), I focus on the powerful belief that you can determine your own course and greatly influence the quality of your life by becoming your own boss. I don't mean you have to leave the company and strike out on your own. Rather, you need to view yourself as the leader of your life, regardless of whether you work for yourself or inside an organization.

Back in 1994, I was a pioneer in the field of executive counseling, which helped individuals zero in on the talents that would help them build new careers. IBM, Digital Equipment Corporation, Wang Laboratories, General Electric, and others had begun dumping white-collar workers by the thousands, and it became clear that our old concepts of loyalty—and our visions of ourselves as being employed by others—were no longer working. So, I began to show my clients how to consider themselves self-employed by developing the kind of personal entrepreneurship that would place them in control of their life.

For the next twelve years, I taught individuals how to balance a new sense of self with the needs of an organization. We focused on how to become more self-directed and independent, as well as on how to collaborate with others. The idea was to prompt my clients to discover their inner economy—and to then find jobs that would allow them to honor their abilities by focusing on what they did best.

The teaching was revolutionary. People started taking their ideas to work and finding new ways to apply their ingenuity. Of course, such initiative shifted the individuals' relationships with the traditional bureaucracy. In fact, when *We Are All Self-Employed* was first published, one disgruntled executive told me, "If I caught my employees reading your book, I'd fire 'em."

In recent years, we've seen what happens when we put our values aside and let ourselves be governed solely by the bottom line. We've watched unscrupulous CEOs go on trial for their misdeeds. We've seen loyal employees walk out the door as they succumb to, and are unprepared for, company layoffs. At the same time, we've witnessed the tidal American job market and said good-bye to the fantasy of predictable and/or endless growth. Brink Lindsey, senior fellow at the Cato Institute, in his March 2004 article "Job Losses and Trade," states, "Even in good times, job losses are an inescapable fact of life in a dynamic market economy. Old jobs are constantly being eliminated as new positions are created."

Our plumber, Dave, once quipped that the only thing that lasts forever is PVC pipe. Dave says archaeologists will unearth PVC a million years from now and find it in pristine condition. Unlike PVC, human beings and organizations change. The job market and global trade are especially volatile, and they'll continue to be so for the foreseeable future. Forrester Research and John McCarthy (leading Forrester's research efforts in China, Hong Kong, Korea, Japan, India, and Australia) in 2002 predicted that, by 2015, 3.3 million U.S. white-collar jobs will have moved offshore to low-wage countries such as India, China, and Mexico—a loss of about 200,000 jobs a year. So, it's time to become adept at reinventing yourself and your relationship to work.

My goal is to help you take on the mind-set of the successfully self-employed and use your gifts in a money-crazed world that keeps changing its demands. This book is for everyone who wants to work smarter, challenge the status quo, strive for quality, find meaningful work while giving back to others, keep on dreaming, and eventually make those dreams come true.

HEY, WAKE UP!

When our daughter, Gabriella, turned 10, she suddenly seemed so tall. As I looked back in the family photo album, I saw Gabriella, at age 5, on Halloween wearing a wedding-dress costume and, at age 7, licking icing off a mixer beater as her mother baked a cake. I realized that more than half of our daughter's life with us was over and that in eight more years she would be off. I vowed to spend more time with her, working on the set of her school play, biking on the weekends, and planning and planting our vegetable garden.

Around that same time, I started exploring wake-up calls with my clients. I asked them to write about the moment when they decided it was time to seize the day and take what they wanted out of life.

"When I turned 35," Yael said, "I asked myself how I felt and the answer was grim. Over the past few years, I've accepted any reasonable job that came along. Reasonable is not joyful. I've come to the conclusion that I'm the only one who can define my interests and then find the work that I love."

Fernando said, "I woke up when the small business I had dedicated myself to for the past three years cracked open like Humpty Dumpty. I did everything I could to save it, working nights and weekends. I thought that just plain working hard was the gateway to my goals. Still, the company crashed and, as a result, I had to look more carefully at the way I was doing business." Fernando joined another firm—part-time—as an account development manager. In his free time, he practiced drumming and worked on recording a CD with his bandmates. Not only were these activities fun, but they gave Fernando the perspective he needed to stand back and analyze what had gone wrong with his company. "That was a valuable time," he said. "I needed to take stock of my strengths and weaknesses and learn more about managing sales and revenues."

Greta, a corporate trainer, grew nostalgic as she walked into my office in a renovated high school. "These old bricks remind me of better times," she said.

"What have you been missing?" I asked.

"For the past seven years, I've been training people who are required to learn. The company mandates training for managers, and many managers are reluctant to sit in a classroom all day. The bricks remind me of happier days, when I worked in an inner-city school. We made it so much fun that our kids really wanted to be there. We planned arts-and-crafts activities, plays, sports, and even water balloon fights."

"Tell me more about that experience."

"I recall two brothers who went home for lunch and came back with half of it on their shirts; a teenage boy, who loved rock 'n' roll and tutored younger students; and the kids who waited for me on their bikes as I drove the last few blocks to school so that they could race me to the parking lot."

"How is this memory a wake-up call for you today?"

"I don't want to go back to an inner-city school," Greta said, "but I do want to work with people who want to learn, and I want to create an environment that encourages them. I've just discovered this desire as I've been talking with you."

The recollection of work that you really loved can lead you in a new direction. But there are other kinds of wake-up calls. A random encounter can cause you to rethink your priorities at work. For example, let's say you come across a homeless man slumped over on a bench. Others pass him by, but your heart opens and you hand him the sandwich you just bought for lunch. You decide you want to make a difference and reach out to others. Helping people will be a primary goal in your next job.

You might also get a wake-up call when a colleague offers unexpected praise. An offhand comment, such as "You have a vivid imagination," may provide the confidence boost you need to pursue a new assignment. Many different experiences can wake you up to who you are and what you need. An experience can be either affirming or unsettling, but the idea is to let it grab you and see where it leads.

REMEMBER, YOU'RE THE BOSS

Today, too many people see themselves as job seekers dependent on the vagaries of the economy. They are waiting—for the market to improve, for someone to tell them what they should do, or for the right job at the right level and salary to appear. "Maybe I'll be lucky," says the job seeker, "and out of three hundred applicants, the employer will select me for an interview." If that describes you, then you hope for the best each time. You cross your fingers, hoping that you'll get placed in the candidate pool, and then pray you'll be the one to get the job. However, the chance that you'll get it is less than one in three hundred—which isn't very promising.

If you are still waiting around for that lucky break, consider the following:

- The economy will continue to churn.

- When the economy is sluggish, it needs your help.

- Waiting in line only results in sore feet and increased frustration.

- If you get "the job," it's going to be temporary.

- You can take charge of your life if you change your thinking from an "employed" to a "self-employed" attitude.

If you choose to be proactive and to stop waiting on good luck, you'll have just promoted yourself. *From now on, you will be the boss.* You'll be responsible for discovering what's in your heart, for reaching out to find satisfying work rather than merely settling, and for managing the tensions that naturally arise when you enter uncharted territory. In the process, you'll have to discover what kinds of support you need from others and what kinds of risks you're prepared to take. Nevertheless, this attitude will allow you to be the prime mover of your life—whether or not you end up reporting to a superior.

If someone were to tell you at this moment, "You are the boss of your own work life," you might feel skeptical and scared, as well as a bit excited. Keep in mind that you don't have to dive into the deep end right away. All I'm asking for is your curiosity. Start to challenge your assumptions about job hunting. Explore what it means to be self-employed and take the lead in the process of your reinvention.

CHALLENGING YOUR ASSUMPTIONS

Often, a job search is tainted by the wrong assumptions—especially by the conventional wisdom that says the bigger the salary, the better the job. When I asked Karolina, a successful sales representative, what she wanted out of life, she exclaimed, "Money matters the most!" as if the answer were obvious.

"Then why have you been out of work for a whole year?" I challenged. She had already turned down sales jobs in related industries because she couldn't "get behind the product." As she sat there, she realized that she was parroting back the culture's value of the importance of money and hadn't fully examined her values and beliefs.

Many of my clients quote from the bible of the outer economy, which views the money machine as its deity. They allow this view to influence all their decisions and most of their career moves. They hire me to help them find better situations, but usually they are struggling with a far more fundamental matter. After a while, their questions lead us to their inner economy—and to their dulled or pitted spirits. They have forfeited enthusiasm for burden, fullness for a sense of unworthiness, and hope for fear. Outer-economy fixes—such as a raise, a promotion, or a new wardrobe—assuage but don't solve the underlying problems.

Feeling financially encumbered and emotionally conflicted, these people are struggling to regain their balance. They have been repeatedly jostled off center by their inability to find meaningful work and to live by the values that matter to them the most. When I ask, "Will you describe the crossroads you have reached in your work life?" I get the following replies:

- "I earn a decent income, and it certainly looks like I have a great job, but something is missing. Will you help me figure out what's wrong?"

- "I've been overfishing the pond and depleting my resources. Can you help me replenish my enthusiasm?"

- "I'm feeling hollow, and work feels empty. Do you think it's too late to discover my passion and put it to good use?"

- "Sometimes I feel good about my job, but, at other times, I'm ambivalent. Is there a way to narrow this gap to more consistently enjoy and be productive in my work?"

- "I know that leaving my company—running away—isn't the solution, but I have a lousy relationship with my boss. Is it possible to shift my thinking and alter this relationship?"

All of these questions relate to the inner economy, which defines how we value ourselves and our place in the world. Such issues are not addressed by books about how to manage your time, write a better resume, or get ahead of the competition. The answer resides in only one place—inside you. Only you know how your human spirit can be expressed—or stifled—by a job.

LIVING THE QUESTIONS

Over the past two decades, I've asked my clients: Are you willing to live in a state of ongoing crisis and just accept what you can get? Will you keep blaming your associates or boss for your unhappiness? Will you jeopardize your organization—including the lives of dedicated employees and their families—because you're afraid to search your soul and confront your demons?

If the answer to these questions is no, I move on to the tougher ones: Will you challenge yourself by opening new doors so that you can find a better way of both engaging your hidden talents and acknowledging the talents of others? Will you wade through anxiety to confront the beliefs that are blocking your progress? Are you ready to grow into another stage of life? Will you take a risk and let your imagination run wild, exploring your passions and writing about your dreams? Do you have the courage to engage the world on your own terms?

There are no right or wrong answers, and it may take some time to come up with honest and heartfelt replies. The point of my inquiry is to help my clients reassess their current expectations and beliefs.

Many of these people have been cut loose from comfortable and secure positions and now have to fend for themselves in a highly competitive job market. I've learned not to be afraid for them but instead to be curious—to listen to their thoughts and view all their questions as part of a life-affirming exploration. For each person, the question that all the searching and discomfort boils down to is this: How can I create my future—take charge of my job and career—to have a more fulfilling life?

My client François said, "I find myself working at jobs where everyone's goal is to make money. While that feeds my family, it does not feed my soul or allow me to feel good about helping the world. Where can I go from here?"

Freedom is earned, not given. It requires hard work and attention. And, it requires that you give yourself permission to explore your gifts and talents. In the process, you may discover a new calling or uncover skills you had forgotten or were compelled to leave behind. The Socratic dictum "Know thyself" is still extremely relevant in our modern pressure-cooker world. As philosopher Joseph Campbell said, "The privilege of a lifetime is being who you are."

FOLLOWING THE RETHINKING WORK® PROCESS

In the remaining chapters, I will lead you through the Rethinking Work process (see illustration on page 16), which consists of three steps that will help you assess your goals and then manifest them in your work. Chapter 2, "The Right to Reflect," offers a model for *reflecting* on who you are and what you want. Chapter 3, "The Permission to Explore," presents a guide for *exploring* your options, networking, and defining the kind of place in which you'd like to work. Chapter 4, "The Courage to Engage," focuses on *engaging* the outer world—testing out your new ideas and making a place for them in the marketplace.

This three-step process will serve you well at many of life's turning points. The need for money will always be a reality, but you will

THE RETHINKING WORK® PROCESS

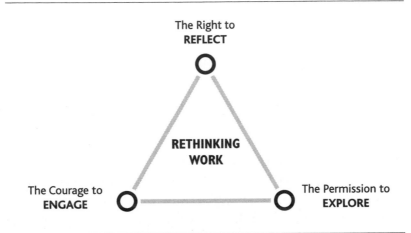

The Right to
REFLECT

**RETHINKING
WORK**

The Courage to
ENGAGE

The Permission to
EXPLORE

no longer need to feel battered by the outer economy or by a host of external values that may not be true for you.

After completing the Rethinking Work process, Bjorn, a portfolio manager, said, "I am moving to a smaller firm where I will be able to put my creativity to work and make things happen. The past year has taught me about myself and about what I need to do to be happy in my work and my life."

Step 1: The Right to REFLECT
Questioning, Observing, Evaluating, and Clarifying

Spirit is what fuels your creativity and your connectedness to work. We often hear people say, "She has a great spirit," or, "His spirit came alive all of a sudden." Sometimes we think, "That idea has no spirit," or, "That company lacks spirit." It is something that we instinctively know is present. Spirit radiates warmth and enthusiasm. It is what keeps us alive and vital and motivated, and everyone knows when it is missing.

Whenever I hit a slump in my work life, I take steps to restore my sunken spirit. It sometimes takes me a while to find the source of my discomfort. However, I intuitively try to do the right thing by going within myself for contemplation and reflection. I notice where the connection between my heart and my head has rusted. I investigate the reason everything feels wrong. I notice that even the most mundane tasks irritate me. I watch the mounting symptoms of low energy—groggily crawling out of bed each morning, spending the day watching the clock, and easily giving in to any slight distraction. When the progression has gone too far, I feel confined and afraid of being trapped. I ask myself, How can I inspire anyone if I'm feeling this flat and out of sorts? My question then becomes even more basic: How can I earn my living in this awful frame of mind?

We all have moments of discouragement and self-doubt, and they have something to teach us. I have learned that our needs and desires shift over time and that we must learn to have compassion for ourselves. So, I take some time to consider my present situation. I try to understand, not judge, my thoughts. I ask, What am I missing? What would make me bound up from the bed to greet my day? What spirit, or quality of life, do I need to cultivate?

No matter what our job is, we all show signs of rust or wear at certain times; but if we take the time to discover what our spirit needs, we can find a way to access it. Then, work will become enjoyable again.

When I take the time to assess who I am and what I want, I am investing in my inner economy. In this way, I begin to rebuild my confidence and restore my energy. I then have the resources I need to earn my keep and serve my clients. I want to pass that lesson on to you and then show you how to move from reflection to the start of seeing tangible results.

I often ask my clients to make a list of the things they feel are missing in their lives. Kirsten, a corporate lobbyist, was feeling discontented and limited by her job. She wrestled with the question, How can I be successful and feel like I am helping others? She began to realize that she wanted to put her skills to work for a particular cause instead of for a company. Deepak, a chief operating officer, was out of sorts because he needed better boundaries. "How can I start saying 'no' more often and still feel that I'm respecting others and their needs?" he asked. As he reflected on his relationship with his department heads, he began working toward a better balance.

Reflecting can also help you see what part of yourself you've put aside to bring home a bigger paycheck. Larry, an organizational consultant, asked, "How do I stop drifting farther and farther away from my values and find my way back home?" He was no longer spending enough time working one-on-one with his clients. He'd become so successful that he spent the bulk of his time managing his business, and he felt cramped by piles of paperwork. The solution was to get back in the field.

A generous salary, raise, or year-end bonus can temporarily ignite your enthusiasm or bring a momentary sense of relief, but only by asking meaningful questions can you decide what qualities you wish to nurture in your work. It is also important to identify what dampens your spirit and makes you long to break free.

Giuseppe, a journalist working for a city newspaper, said, "My boss had a sign above his desk that read, 'Beatings will continue until morale improves.' The culture was ruled by fear. We weren't allowed to ask questions. If I hadn't been reporting and away from my desk most of the time, I never would have survived that atmosphere.

Finally, I realized that whenever I came to work, I left my spirit out-side the door. In the past, I would sing or hum as I wrote my stories, but that wasn't happening anymore. So, after five years, I joined another paper and, to my surprise, I began to sing again."

The process of reflection encourages us to listen to our discon-tent and remember what it was like when work was good. Chapter 2, "The Right to Reflect," provides simple journal exercises to lead you through this step and help you get to know yourself.

Step 2: The Permission to EXPLORE
Researching, Seeking, Experimenting, Sorting, and Connecting

The biggest mistake you can make is to believe you work for someone else. Ultimately, we are accountable not to an organization or to a twist in the economy but to ourselves.

The second-biggest mistake is staying a prisoner of routine and remaining encased in your current world. To create your future, you need to become an explorer with the mission of determining what you know and what you don't. I have told my clients, "Your reflec-tions won't bear fruit if you try to move them out into the world too fast. You need an in-between step to help you explore a full range of options before you take your new ideas out into the marketplace."

You need time to explore how you can put your skills to use, to test how they might be received, and to figure out whether your plan needs any refinements. You also need time to see whether the move you are considering is right for you—whether it truly represents your next phase of growth and the values you wish to contribute to the world.

Lisa was a psychology major who got a job teaching first and sec-ond graders at a private school. She also loved clothing design. So, the goal she arrived at was to combine psychology with fashion by helping women dress for success. Her plan appeared sound, and when she was offered a job as a sales associate at her favorite boutique, she jumped at the chance. But, it turned out that she had little in common with the staff—and she hated the competition around ringing up sales. Lisa's primary interest was in assessing the image the customer was trying to project and then recommending wardrobe changes to both reflect that customer's personality and enhance her self-esteem. Lisa realized that she had leapt too quickly. She needed to spend more time in the exploring phase to test her expectations against reality.

In the exploring phase, you need to be like Sherlock Holmes and ruthlessly look for holes in your central thesis. This phase takes patience and the ability to run through different scenarios in your mind. I tell my clients this is the time to stand back, analyze the situation, and gather all the facts—rather than to charge forward like a superhero. Whereas the superhero leaps into action, the detective watches and waits. The detective is ever vigilant and extremely rigorous, and looks at the problem from all sides. If this process takes you back to your basics, that is okay. As Holmes would say, "I can't make bricks without clay."

Keiko, the deputy director of a nonprofit organization, returned from her vacation to find a pink slip on her desk. By the next afternoon, she had started the exploring process. She said, "I have better qualifications than ever to lead a nonprofit organization, but I could go in either of two directions: general management or fund-raising."

Like most people who lose their job, Keiko wanted to get back on track as quickly as possible. "Be patient," I said. "Don't send out a wave of resumes this week. Take the time to consider all your strengths. Give yourself permission to explore the work world. Talk with others who are working in the kinds of jobs you think you'd like and see what the pluses and minuses are. Then, trust your gut to tell you whether this type of work is right for you."

Luka, a venture capitalist and amateur chef, started the exploring process and found a way to combine his financial acumen with his love for food. He discovered that many restaurants needed help managing their assets. So, he created a business named Food Ventures and started out by offering financial consulting to a local restaurant on a pro bono basis. He also helped the owner create a unique and profitable menu that increased the customer base and financed an expansion to a second site. While still working at his day job, Luka capitalized on this success to attract his first paying client.

It's not enough to just think about creativity and all your great ideas. You must identify the particular skills that will be useful to a broader audience. You must find a forum in which to express your creativity and then give it a trial run.

"I think of my career path as tracking toward an unseen goal that lies over the horizon," says Aziz, a corporate executive who is in the process of launching himself as a consultant. "It's often better to slightly bend your life by making little changes that will bring you closer to your true path. One success will give you the confidence to take another step. The goal of the exploring process is to keep your balance and not give in to inertia and impatience."

In Chapter 3, "The Permission to Explore," I will show you how making a series of small adjustments can help you reach your goal.

Step 3: The Courage to ENGAGE
Focusing, Acting, Launching, Selling, and Innovating

Some people have a sweet tooth for taking action. They rush toward their finish line before they test their assumptions. That is why the final phase—bringing your dream out into the world—involves learning the art of refining and adjusting your goals to ensure that your new plan will succeed.

This is the time to go over the details of your grand design and see whether everything is in place to support it. As Lily Tomlin said, "I always wanted to be somebody, but I should have been more specific."

As I began to write this book, I looked up from my desk when I heard the clop, clop, clop of 10,000 pounds of stone being dumped onto my neighbor's lawn. Later that day, I examined the grayish-brown heap and felt impressed at the variety of the stones—flat rectangles, irregular squares, cantaloupe-sized spheres, and triangular wedges. The next day, Christophe, the mason, dug a two-foot-wide, six-inch-deep ditch along the property's edge and laid a pea-gravel foundation in the trough. Then, he eyed the pile of rocks and began to select just the right ones for his needs.

I felt deeply satisfied observing Christophe's methodical, even-paced style as he built a seventy-five-foot-long wall that hugged the street and then curved around, like a boomerang, to embrace the yard. And, I learned a great deal about the art of turning a vision into a reality.

Before Christophe engaged in work each day, he would step back and assess the wall for the perfect fit, or placement, of new rock. This process of stepping back has been very useful to my clients, too. I told this story to Jordan as she struggled to find "the big picture" and identify the key elements of her design.

Jordan worked for an insurance company while earning her MBA, but she wasn't sure what direction to take after graduation. She knew that she wanted to work with people as well as develop her business acumen. So, at the insurance company, she volunteered to help the human resources staff and began learning about benefits, compensation, administrative and technical systems, training, and recruitment. She had good rapport with the recruiting director and found that she especially liked assisting in the hiring process.

After a year, Jordan applied for a job as a researcher on a special task force that consisted of managers and executives. She loved her sense of purpose and independence, but when the company was sold to a larger enterprise, Jordan didn't find the merger at all appealing. It was time for her to step back and identify the key elements of her next career move. Jordan came up with a number of elements she wanted her next job to involve: recruiting, research, contact with customers, more compensation, making a difference in people's lives, a collaborative atmosphere with minimal office politics, a commute of twenty-five minutes or less, and the flexibility to work from home.

Jordan wasn't sure whether she wanted to work in corporate human resources or in an executive search firm, so she lined up several informational interviews and also contacted people who had been helpful in her previous position. She asked, Would you tell me about how you use your day? Would you walk me through how you do your work? What most excites you about working for this company?

Networking can help you choose the elements that contribute the most to your overall design. Jordan's interviews helped her discover the kind of work she was best suited for. After three months, she had narrowed down her options and decided to look for a research post in an executive search firm. A company in New York soon offered her a job with a salary and a biannual bonus. Jordan had only a twenty-five-minute commute as well as the option to work from home. All of the major elements of her design were now securely in place.

RETHINKING WORK AS A LIFELONG JOURNEY

The purpose of using the Rethinking Work process is to increase the possibility and frequency of feeling genuinely happy and connected to your work. Rethinking Work is an ongoing process, not just a one-time thing. Life is a never-ending journey, and you have to keep choosing the path that presents the greatest interest.

At some point, you may find yourself feeling a little stale and disconnected. But, once you start this process, things will begin to shift. You may wake up in the middle of the night, write down some sudden inspiration, and realize that a whole new range of possibilities lies before you. This is when you may think, There aren't enough hours in the day for me to do everything I'd like to do!

Remember that you don't have to keep taking half-baked assignments or hopping from interview to interview. Once you wake up to the fact that life is fleeting—that you have only a limited time to make your contribution—you can clarify your strengths and decide what it is that you really want. Although you'll never resolve all of your challenges, things will work out for the best on the whole. You may begin to engage in a spirited, if not necessarily perfect, dialogue with people in your current company—which will allow you to bring a different set of skills into play. Or, you may find new opportunities in the job market that will allow you to forge a new relationship with the business world. Either way, you'll come out ahead.

THE RIGHT TO REFLECT

WHAT MAKES YOU UNIQUE?

Know thyself.
SOCRATES

When I was in my late 30s, I felt as if I had come to a dead end. Each day, I woke up and asked, How can I breathe new life into my career? Where can I get fresh air? I wanted to bounce out of bed and feel happy about how I was going to invest my time and other resources that day. Earning a good living was important to me, but I ached to be in love with work again—to enjoy the day-to-day experience and not just the material rewards.

My Socratic process went like this: Do I really want to continue running a successful executive search business? If not, what on earth will I do next? I put on my coat, anticipating that a walk in the brisk winter air would be just the thing to clear my thoughts. After a few

THE RETHINKING WORK® PROCESS

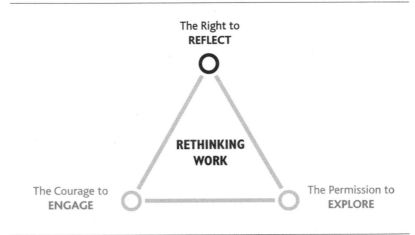

The Right to
REFLECT

**RETHINKING
WORK**

The Courage to
ENGAGE

The Permission to
EXPLORE

blocks, I stopped at a local newsstand. My eyes popped when I spotted the question on the cover of the December 1986 *Esquire:* "What are you doing with the rest of your life?"

The cover story, "Cooling Out," by *Esquire* editor Philip Moffitt, was accompanied by a photograph of a man stuck in a revolving door. The picture captured my feeling of being trapped. I imagined myself in that door, controlled and pushed by others' needs and demands. I kept wishing that my customers, employees, and colleagues would stop shoving at the door so I could step out on the pavement.

At that moment, the proverbial lightbulb turned on and I realized I had to free myself. The only way to escape that revolving door was to push hard, make a mad leap, and jump free of it. Over the next few weeks, I took a very bold step. I closed my executive search practice to launch Rethinking Work, a firm in which I would create a new platform for career consulting. In a sense, I was my own first client.

My goal was to help people find more meaning in their work; but, first, I had to find more meaning in mine.

I had saved enough money to live on for about six months. However, my question to myself, "How do I engage my spirit at work?" was mystifying to others and seemed to me, at times, to embody a vain and selfish pursuit. When my colleagues said, "You're crazy to give up your business!" they stoked my insecurity. Friends reminded me of the years I had worked to build a profitable business. I looked at those same years and felt that I had created a profitable trap. It was as though I had already quit working and was just showing up at the office. Whenever I listened to my inner voice, I knew that I could not sustain my success—despite external accolades and generous compensation. The only thing that really mattered was to feel alive and engaged again.

It was not just the passion I missed but also the climb to success. I had created the business, hired the staff, selected the equipment, found new clients, and built a reputation. A few years later, with all those accomplishments behind me, I found myself simply maintaining an ongoing enterprise. When I reflected on this, my inner voice (which was becoming quite talkative) said, Look for another mountain to climb.

I noticed, too, the frequency with which I asked myself, How will I make as much money as before? Occasionally during the transition period, a company would call and announce that it had just hired one of my candidates. Each time I'd think, I must be off my rocker to close down this business. I'd feel happy for the candidate—but envious as well. By then, I was sure it was time for me to heed my own advice and tend to my renewal.

When I looked at the *Esquire* article again, I noticed a second picture: a photograph of a door that had been left slightly ajar. Here was the opening, the chance for the reader to decide: What do I really want? and, What gifts do I have to offer others? These were the questions that led to the next stage of my adventure.

REALIZING THAT WORK IS PERSONAL

I began to understand that work is personal, so I started asking my clients, What kind of work puts a smile on your face? Are you doing that kind of work? If you did something you truly love, how might your life be better? If more people were happy on the job, how might the world be better?

You can be a mechanic, pilot, hairdresser, chemist, boat builder, child care provider, tax attorney, cattle rancher, or musician. What matters is that you feel connected to your work. Ask yourself, Am I expressing myself and giving my gifts to others? Am I doing something that energizes me?

I don't want to send you on a quixotic quest for the perfect job. I do want to encourage you to find your own truth and then take your essence to work. In this way, you'll not only be serving others and feeling more joyful, but you'll be earning a living at it.

Melissa wanted to retreat from her very public role in the health care field. At 58, she was a CEO of a nonprofit organization who was feeling tired and worn down. "I figured it was time to get over my adrenaline addiction and find a less demanding job," she said. "So, I joined this organization thinking that I could run it without too many glitches and then retire early."

"How is your plan working?" I asked.

"Not very well," she said. "In the past, I always had a strong emotional attachment to my work. I was spearheading major health and medical reforms in large cities. My skills were well used; I was busy and admired. Now, my effort to retreat has backfired. I don't believe in the mission of this organization and, as a result, I'm not so sure my colleagues believe in me."

"So, how do you feel?" I asked.

"Bored, stuck, fearful, and angry. I'm lonely for peers who are smart and edgy. Really, I'm disappointed in myself and realize that I need to care again."

"What do you mean by 'care again'?"

"I don't want to give up on chasing something I believe in. I want work that excites me. In this role, I'm losing energy. I thought that, with your counsel, I might go into fund-raising, advocacy, or lobbying in Washington. But, I'm not sure which organization I'd like to work for."

For the next six months, Melissa continued working in her present job while reflecting on the qualities she valued in her work. She told me stories about her most satisfying accomplishments and about the kind of corporate culture that invigorated her. We also talked about what was happening in her personal life. One common theme emerged as a primary concern—caring for her aging parents—and led Melissa to a new vocation.

"Originally, my focus was on some mechanical role, such as fund-raising or grant writing, but I've discovered that I need to direct my energy toward a cause I admire," Melissa concluded. "I can't just look for a new job. I need to begin with something that is dear to my heart."

"What have you discovered as you've reflected on your stories and our conversations?" I asked.

"I wrote several articles about caring for my parents. I also negotiated with my siblings about how we would accomplish this enormous undertaking, share the tasks, and try to stay healthy in the process. I've been thinking about putting together programs and seminars for Baby Boomers and their aging parents, with a focus on the well-being of both groups of people. Who knows, maybe I'll even write a book!"

"You seem so excited and knowledgeable when you talk about this area. Look at you; you're beaming!"

Melissa's journey reminds us that our values always play the most important role. As Paulo Coelho wrote in *The Alchemist*, "Remember that wherever your heart is, there you will find your treasure." After you find your treasure, everything you have learned along the way will have new meaning—and your life will make more sense.

HUNGERING FOR MEANINGFUL WORK

While listening to my clients, I thought a great deal about people's hunger for meaningful work. Each day, we sit down to a job just as we might sit down to dinner. The trouble is, most of us have no control over the menu. So, we pick a little here and there. We eat what others have prepared, and not much of it is to our liking. We eat but still feel hungry because we haven't found the things we really crave.

As the thirteenth-century Sufi poet Rumi said, "People don't look at themselves, and so they blame one another." When the work menu is tedious or difficult, we start blaming the boss, our colleagues, or some poor, unwitting family member for our sour mood. Reflecting is therefore a fundamentally moral act—because it requires us to take responsibility for ourselves.

I also tell my clients that they can't feed their spirit if they keep focusing on externals, such as conventional career moves and other people's expectations. They have to know what it is that they hunger for, and to figure it out, they have to look within.

Luisa was advancing in her company. She had moved up from a manager of human resources to that department's director but, in the process, she forgot to ask the most important question: What kind of work am I best suited for? In her mind's eye, she was destined to sit at the executive strategy table, so she focused on winning the top job. Yet, during the interview process, she had neglected to talk with the department managers about what they wanted and needed. It turned out that they wanted a director who would maximize operations and address recruitment, compensation, and management development. However, this nitty-gritty wasn't what Luisa had in mind. She complained that the hiring committee had held back vital information and that they should have known about her aspirations.

If you base your beliefs about change on external values, you will think only about what others are supposed to do and give. You will expect employers to read your mind and offer you the opportunities you feel are the most pivotal to your future.

Transition is never just black and white. To find out what you're meant to do, you have to endure some initial confusion and then explore the territory. The actual change comes last. You "arrive" as you become more confident and focused on your goals. Before you land the right position, you may need to consider a wide range of job choices and investigate a few of them thoroughly.

When Kevin lost his job as vice president of finance in a midsize manufacturing firm, he panicked. Instead of reflecting on what he really wanted, he took the first job that came along when a friend offered him similar work and parallel compensation if he would be willing to move out of state. Three weeks into the job—after leaving his family behind—Kevin realized that his unexamined, fear-driven choice was not a change at all. Furthermore, he had an impossible weekend commute. He missed his family, and for what? He was still stuck on the same rung of the career ladder. The process of reflecting could have saved him from this misstep.

Reflection can also help you transform the job you have right now. Carmella, the president of a jewelry manufacturing company, complained, "The executive team that reports to me is fractured. We're name-calling and avoiding face-to-face meetings. Can you help us get back together so we can enjoy our work again?" After interviewing six executives by telephone, I met the scowling group in person and began by saying, "The goal will not be victory (win-lose) but agreement (win-win). First, we'll all need to learn to respect one another. Doing so involves carefully considering our thoughts, words, and deeds. Only by reflecting on our personal responsibilities—in other words, by facing ourselves—can we strengthen the communication and relationships necessary to unite and grow this company."

My strategy was to create a safe context in which the executives could talk openly about their feelings and reflect on how their working relationships might change for the better. After a significant outburst, one team member said, "I can't stand all this hostility. We're like kids who are playing very badly. We need a time-out." This comment marked the turning point. After the time-out, one person admitted to the group that he had been brash and rude and would do everything possible from then on to choose his words more carefully. The team established a new rule: Think before you speak—in other words, reflect on your part in the problem—and then share your part of the solution.

Carmella had raised the fundamental question, How can we stop this cycle of blame and lead the company forward? She asked the team members to take responsibility for their actions—but first she addressed her actions. She said, "I've made some blind choices and also pointed the finger. I need to listen better to your feedback, weigh all of your suggestions, and then make a decision for the good of all."

Reflecting on who you are and what matters most to you is the key to your success. Looking at life from the inside out allows you to make better choices. Dana Reeve, who helped her husband, Christopher Reeve, through a paralyzing spinal injury and later faced her own lung cancer with dignity and calmness, made this perspective the topic of her 2004 commencement address at Middlebury College. She said, "Some choices will choose you. How you face these choices, these turns in the road, with what kind of attitude, more than the choices themselves, is what will define the context of your life."

BECOMING AWARE OF THE OUTER-DIRECTED VS. THE INNER-DIRECTED ATTITUDE

The following table will help you determine whether your attitude is primarily outer directed or inner directed.

An outer-directed attitude can lead you to walk another's path. Then, someday, you'll look back and see that you missed opportunities to walk your path. An outer-directed attitude can also cause you to stay in a job because it exemplifies the path everyone expected you to follow. Such an attitude can keep you stuck on someone else's path indefinitely.

Consider Ralph, who's discontented with his role as a sales manager. He started to look for an alternative, but, in the end, he lost

OUTER- VS. INNER-DIRECTED ATTITUDES

OUTER-DIRECTED ATTITUDE	**INNER-DIRECTED ATTITUDE**
• What others think about me is most important.	• Knowing myself creates the opportunity to both consider what others say and to attend to my own spirit.
• My degree, credentials, and job history guarantee my next move and my happiness.	• History can help to guide my future, although at every juncture in my career, I owe it to myself to search my heart, clarify my values, and review my options.
• I job hunt as though I'll be lucky to find a job.	• I ask myself, "What gives me joy? What stirs my passion?"
• I ignore personal renewal and take a new job thinking that any change will be for the better.	• I have been deepening my regard for myself and allowing myself to grow and contribute from the heart.

heart and took a similar job, thinking, Hey, it's the devil I know. An outer-directed attitude makes it easy to settle—to squelch your feelings and your responsibility to yourself. In this state of mind, you'll take a job that puts you right back where you started. An inner-directed attitude, on the other hand, keeps you in control.

Traversing Peaks and Valleys

An outer-directed career produces a series of lofty peaks and dismal valleys. You will find scant level ground and, at times, the going can be rough even for the fittest mountaineer. When I asked Luc, who was in his mid-30s, to draw a line depicting his work history over the past seven years, the lows were deep and the highs were sharp and fleeting (see the figure below). Luc had allowed himself to be buffeted about by his employer's expectations and by economic shifts rather than look at his needs and decision-making process.

Stop now and chart your work history. See what the lows have in common and what you were feeling when you reached the highs. Ask yourself these questions:

- At what point did my satisfaction come from within (signifying an inner-directed attitude)? At what point was I motivated by outside forces (signifying an outer-directed attitude)?

- Does some crossroad exist at which these two attitudes meet?

- Is the overall pattern one that I want to perpetuate?

- How can I change the picture so that I'll be happier?

Luc's Work History

Don't worry if your answer to the last question is a little sketchy. The goal is to help you see your pattern and tune in to the ways you might change it for the better.

After completing this exercise, Anne, a marketing manager, confessed, "I did just about everything I possibly could during the past several years to avoid this kind of self-awareness. Reflection was something I dreaded. With the clock ticking, I've finally started to look inside myself to uncover the roots of my unhappiness, to know and appreciate my strengths, and to get what I want."

To achieve your goals, you need to keep a keen eye on the outside world—current events, business news, and sector-specific information. You also need a clear inner vision to channel your power and move toward the kind of life you want. Adopting others' passions and trying to conform to conventional expectations will only result in your settling for or holding on to the status quo as if it were some kind of magic talisman. It is far better to reflect on what you need, set an appropriate course, and take your chances in the current moment.

It's time to ask yourself, How many times did I concentrate on packaging myself with a fancy brochure or a crisp new resume before discovering what I really wanted? You may have pitched yourself very well, but getting the job or sealing the deal didn't bring you the fulfillment or sense of adventure you were seeking. You felt yourself fading a little bit each time you fell short of who you were or who you could be.

The issue now is not the job fit or how you market your credentials. It's not about the organization's challenges or the customer's needs. (The organization's concern is rightfully about meeting payroll and gaining market share.) No one else is going to put your survival or your aspirations in the number one position. You have to identify and then start looking out for what you need.

OPENING NEW DOORS

I try to avoid the notion that we have to begin all over again. We don't have the time, energy, or money to keep starting from scratch. Instead, we can retrace our careers to search for the skills with "recycle value" and find the treasures buried in our past. This effort involves not only closing the doors to situations that no longer work for us but considering the doors we might reopen. In other words, we can sort through our history for meaningful experiences, contacts, and expertise and explore the opportunities we passed up. As we do this, we may find many interests that are worth reviving.

Several decades ago, I inherited from my grandparents a gooseneck lamp with a green glass shade. The scratched base, frayed cord, tarnished brass, and mottled shade showed little promise to the casual observer. My siblings ignored the lamp, whereas I saw its character. Now, more than thirty years later, that lamp illuminates the foyer of my home and has become a conversation piece.

Restoration is a subject I broach continually in my work. I ask my clients to write about their history, starting with their family background and then noting the high and low points of their life, the major turning points, and how they came to their current work situation. All of them end up submitting at least a few pages. Some produce a lot more, finding themselves absorbed in their narrative. I call this exercise the mini-autobiography.

William Shakespeare said, "The web of our life is of mingled yarn." We make wise career decisions while tending to the overall tapestry of our life, considering both personal and work experiences. Our attitude toward our partner, children, community, leisure time, aging parents, and financial obligations is as important as the type of work we're drawn to. As Jeffrey, an attorney, said, "I performed an analysis of the business I was interested in buying by generating a five-year projection of what it would cost to develop it. At the last minute, however, I realized that I hadn't discussed the venture with my wife. I wouldn't have been able to accomplish much without her understanding and support!"

After we unravel their mini-autobiography, I ask my clients, Has your writing reopened any doors? Here are some of their responses:

- "Looking back, I see that I was happiest when working with mission-driven people to perform an important community service."

- "I especially like problem solving, coaching others to help them grow, and facilitating outcomes that are not easily reached."

- "My high points? The times that I said whatever I felt was true and real and authentic to my mission and myself."

- "I feel passion for the period in my 20s that I spent in Colombia and for the possibility of now returning to a similar place. Although I can't return to South America with my family, I would like to find a situation that involves dealing with the Latino community."

My client Sandra worked as a grant writer in the health care field and pursued quilting as a pastime. "I learned a great deal from writing this mini-autobiography," she said. " I have a creative side and an analytical side, and I like to feed them both. If I neglect one for the sake of the other, I'm not happy."

Sandra also realized that she felt hampered by family patterns and obligations. "I've been unable to generate any enthusiasm about applying for nursing jobs," she said, "because that was my father's path. He became a doctor because his father insisted on it, and he was stressed about his work throughout his life. My mother encouraged him to do something else, but soon they had a large family and he spent his life feeling trapped. Lately, I've been feeling trapped, too. I ask myself, What work have I done—either paid or unpaid—that I find rewarding?"

Sandra began investigating the feasibility of earning a living through her hands-on skill and interest in home crafts. "The line of work that pays the best and contains a lot of openings is ceramic tile installation," she said. "This work is just like patchwork quilting, one of my first loves."

Sandra interviewed with the senior manager of a tile installation company. He was impressed with both her knowledge of ceramic tiling and her references, which included an architect for whom she had tiled three bathrooms twelve years earlier. The manager offered her work as a subcontractor. Sandra discovered that she could make $40 per hour and often more, and her meeting was so successful that it led to her first job.

"I'm sore all over from two days of intensive manual labor but grinning from ear to ear," Sandra reported. "This job entailed a high-end Italian-marble bathroom installation in a luxury brownstone in the city. The client was very particular about the look he wanted to achieve, asking us to remove the tiles he had installed just two months ago. I let him sort through the tiles himself and choose the ones he liked best. It took a bit longer to finish the job than I had originally anticipated, but it was top-quality work and he was thrilled. He'll be giving a positive report to the tile company."

The process of reflection can help us target certain skills that translate well to other occupations. For example, quilters are often inspired by tile and mosaic work. The tile installation process requires on-the-spot problem solving, measuring and calculating, maintaining good customer relations, and upholding high standards of craftsmanship. Many of Sandra's competencies were needed for this job. As one of her quilting buddies said, "Way cool—now you get to quilt on walls."

COMPOSING YOUR MINI-AUTOBIOGRAPHY

"When I looked over my life, I discovered that I'd thrown away real passions," said Mark Levy, a client who is now a well-known author (*Magic for Dummies* and *Tricks with Your Head*). "Because I hadn't set the world on fire with those passions, I figured they weren't worth pursuing. One was magic. The other was writing. However, I hadn't performed magic tricks in seventeen years and I'd done precious little writing. Nevertheless, when I started to get back into these pursuits, I found myself having so much fun that I decided to combine them. Now, I write about magic!"

If you take the time to write a mini-autobiography, I guarantee that some magic will be waiting for you, too. Start by considering the following points:

- What kind of family did you grow up in? What were the main interests?

- Were your talents and skills encouraged?

- List the high points of your life—the moments that gave you the most fulfillment, excitement, or pleasure.

- List the times when you felt the greatest sense of disappointment.

- Describe the path that brought you to your present job.

- What do you like most about this job?

- What do you like least?

- What brings you to this crossroads in your life today?

RECOGNIZING THAT YOUR TIME IS LIMITED

"I keep reminding myself how short and precious life is," says Dominik, a 54-year-old economist. "Often, I ask myself, When I am about to die, what will I regret not having done with my time? And, if I don't start doing it now, then when?"

Write down all the things you want to accomplish before you die. Then, every morning for the next few weeks, review your list. In time, you may develop the courage to tackle one of your dreams. When I talk with people like Dominik, they often ask me, "Why am I so restless and dissatisfied? Can you help me find my center?" I respond with another set of questions:

- What do you want less of in your life?

- What do you want more of?

- Why are you so tired?

- What qualities do you want to use that you have been ignoring?

ROUNDING OUT THE PICTURE

It's important to consider how your professional life intersects with your personal life as you write your mini-autobiography. Ask yourself these questions:

- How does my work affect my family and social life?

- How does the work I do help others or bring me into a relationship with a larger community?

- How much leisure time do I want and need?

- What are my current baseline financial obligations?

SETTING YOUR SPIRIT FREE

The process of information gathering calls for another important element. Make a list of the doors that you want to close as well as those that you want to open. The following table shows some common responses from my clients.

Which doors do you need to close because the room has grown too stifling? Which do you want to open because they set your spirit free? Write your answers on the doors in the figure on page 44.

What's Behind That Door?

"I've become increasingly unhappy with my firm," said Edward, an accountant. "I've been shutting my office door, and I even moved my desk into one of the corners of the room."

"What exactly are you shutting out?" I asked.

"I no longer agree with the way my firm bills and manages its clients. Our rates are way too high and our clients' needs are changing. I did my best to reexamine our values and our procedures with the company founders. I developed a strategic plan to update our daily operations, but I only got lip service and no real encouragement. My door is shut because I want to close out the firm's dog-

CLOSING AND OPENING DOORS

DOORS TO CLOSE	DOORS TO OPEN
Jumping prematurely. Trying to force people and events to change.	**Having patience.** Staying present, listening, and giving opportunities a chance to grow.
Saying "yes" too often. Making everything equally important; setting few limits and boundaries.	**Saying "no" when necessary.** Establishing a focus and a means to achieve what's most important to me.
Imitating what others have done. Only hoping to do true, sustaining work.	**Creating fresh ideas.** Incorporating who I am and what I'd like to contribute.
Living for the future. Believing that tomorrow's goals are more important than the present moment.	**Relishing today.** Doing the best that I can for now and trusting that a promising future will unfold.
Maintaining an "I can do anything" attitude. Listing my attributes, competencies, and experiences with no particular focus.	**I enjoy and do *x* best.** Specifying a vision that both resonates with my spirit and serves a marketplace need.

matic beliefs and also to hide my frustration, boredom, and apathy. I long for a change, and if it's grown a little uncomfortable in here, I guess it's because I've created a hothouse of sorts in which I've been formulating my plans for the future."

What doors will I open?	What doors will I close?

"Heat has to go somewhere," I said, "and frustration, boredom, and apathy do not necessarily signify failure. Has your hothouse been productive? Has it opened any doors?"

"Oh, yes," Edward said. "After hours, I'm the silent partner in the development of a housing project. Adam, my partner, has an energetic, sales-oriented personality. I serve as the other half: the strategic planner, calm advisor, and constructor of detailed deals."

Self-imposed exile can serve a purpose, but the key is not remaining in the hothouse for too long. Edward carefully crafted his exit from the firm so as to preserve his relationships with the founders, his connections with his colleagues, and his association with his clients. The network he had built would prove useful in his next endeavor. As a housing developer, he would not only open new doors but build them, too.

When No Door Remains in Sight

After I stepped off the bus one day in Harvard Square, a gentleman approached to ask me for directions. We walked together toward the post office, and I commented on his accent. "I'm Russian," he said. My curiosity stirred, I asked how he liked living in the United States.

"Too may choices abound in America!" he responded. "It is difficult to find work." He pointed to all the traffic and the people and continued, "Here, life is go, go, go, but I don't know where to go. In Russia, the government gave me a job. I knew where I was going."

I thought of this man some years later when I helped Wendy, a teacher and jazz musician, pursue her performing career. Wendy said, "My friends and colleagues often ask me how I keep everything going in my life and still play my music. I tell them that it's easy if you're doing what you really, really want and you have a goal. The hard part is figuring all that out!"

I think the Russian man would have agreed with Wendy that figuring it all out is the toughest part. Wendy had the advantage of not only believing in the American Dream but also having spent years assessing and articulating her likes, dislikes, skills, values, and aptitudes. She knew that if she left her decisions to the outer economy—the money-crazed world—she would have to forfeit the chance of ever playing her music.

I tell my clients, "If you can identify your prize, you can then offset the go, go, go imperative of modern life with your core wisdom. Instead of facing a blank wall, you will find new doors."

IDENTIFYING YOUR HIGHEST VALUE

I often hand my clients a deck of one hundred value cards that I've put together over the years and ask them to choose the ones that appeal to them the most. From the pack, they can choose values such as cooperation, community, a quiet place to work, excitement, order, power, mentoring, and friendship. Other values that have proved important to my clients include: feeding the body, mind, and spirit; making a difference in the world; using specific abilities; connecting with others; living in the present; maintaining personal integrity; and expressing oneself.

To clarify what matters most to you, you don't need to work with cards or preexisting lists. You can start by simply writing down the qualities you deem most important in your work and your daily life. Knowing your primary values can help you build self-esteem, clarify your focus, identify your strengths, confidently express your objectives, and discern whether a particular partner or work environment is the right one for you.

My client Kwan, an insurance broker, succeeded in identifying nine important values:

- Experiencing change and variety
- Helping others
- Feeling that my life counts
- Balancing work and play
- Having tranquility on the job
- Preserving stability and order
- Becoming a whole person

- Achieving results

- Working with a team

It would be impossible to explore all nine of these values in a job interview. Hiring committees ask about primary skills, previous jobs, and records of credentials and awards. "We've got to hone these down," I told Kwan. "Instead of taking a broad approach, try to identify the one value that you cherish the most." I gave Kwan a hint: Omit any value that could be considered a subset of another. He sat back and whittled the list down to five. First, he chose "Becoming a whole person" over "Achieving results" based on the rationale that if he became a whole person, he would achieve results. Then, by eliminating duplicates, he condensed his list to

- Becoming a whole person

- Helping others

- Balancing work and play

- Preserving stability and order

- Working with a team

After sharing his list with me, Kwan realized, "At 46, and with three school-age children, I can no longer make choices or view life through a 20-something lens. I feel as though I'm looking through a kaleidoscope and continually turning it to rearrange the pieces— family commitments, mortgage payments, the care of aging parents and in-laws, college-tuition savings, activities for staying healthy, and involvement in school activities. Updating my life design at this stage would be extremely complicated."

"Do you still think you need to change your job at this time?" I probed.

"Yes and no," he said. "Will I die if I don't love my work? The answer is no. But, I do want my boys to see their dad as a happy person who's working hard to achieve his goals."

Finally, I asked Kwan to pick the most important value on his list.

"I do value working with a team," he said, "and I'm going to try to balance work and play in my life. But, becoming a whole person is unquestionably the prize. It's the one value that drives all the others and that will endure throughout my life."

Kwan is now exploring types of work that stretch him beyond his conventional role. His goal is to train other executives and help them increase their creative options.

Other clients note that their values have changed over the past few years. Often, one that they've been nurturing for a while in second or third place has jumped into the lead. When I asked Whitney, a programmer and a sculptor, to complete the values exercise, she was amazed at her discovery. Her top five values surfaced as

- **Creativity:** Finding a twist or an original way to put things together

- **Closeness with my family:** Actively participating in pursuits with my husband and children

- **Spirituality:** Deepening meaningfulness by connecting with others in life

- **Sexuality:** Enjoying my husband's companionship

- **A feeling that my life counts:** Creating something of significance and leaving it to others

Whitney found it difficult to take any of these values off her list. I said, "Maybe you don't have to. But, do you see a common thread?"

Whitney said, "All of my values concern being in the present and making a connection. I'm curious, though, what does working as a programmer have to do with making a connection? Mostly, I work alone."

"Maybe, in your mind's eye, you're connecting to the customers, or users, as you write a program. Alternatively, this value may be developing more importance in your life."

"Yes," Whitney said, "you're absolutely right. My desire is to cut back on my programming and bring my sculpture into the world. I want to connect with people by selling my work at galleries and lecturing at schools, colleges, and, possibly, museums."

Once you begin the process of reflection, you'll discover that it has its own momentum. You may suddenly realize that it costs you less to change and grow than to keep supporting your unhappiness. As author Anaïs Nin once wrote, "And the day came when the risk it took to remain inside the bud was more painful than the risk it took to blossom."

TAKING STOCK OF YOUR INNER ECONOMY

Reflection is vital to our lives. As M. Scott Peck said in *The Road Less Traveled,* "Problems do not go away. They must be worked through or else they remain, forever a barrier to the growth and development of the spirit."

Leonard, 51, lost an executive position and was interviewing for corporate jobs. "During my last interview, the hiring manager asked me point-blank whether I could meet the challenges of the post," he said. "Suddenly, I felt my competitive energy surge. I spewed out tons of reasons why I should be hired. However, on my way home, I realized that a gap existed between what I had said and what dwelled in my heart. Although it appeared that I wanted the job, really I was skeptical."

"What were you unsure about?" I asked.

"I'm not certain that I want to do this kind of work. When I searched within myself, I knew that my rant concerned power—being on top—which to me means earning a healthy paycheck and receiving recognition from the company."

"So, the drives of the outer economy, such as financial reward and competitive triumph, had taken the lead. But, when you checked in with your inner economy, another story emerged."

"That's right," Leonard said. "I've reached a point in my life where I can't go just for the money and the perks. I need to consider my gut values. Making a difference on this planet has become more important to me."

"What if you'd been offered the job?"

"I suppose I would have been temporarily gratified. But, I would also have felt that I'd sold out. The question would have remained: What might I do to earn a living that feels more aligned with who I am?"

Once again, we come back to our central theme. Two economies exist that can inform and guide our decision making, and we can reach a sense of balance only if we address them both. Remember that the inner economy represents a person's heart and soul—his or her authenticity. It embodies who we are when we create our vision. The outer economy represents the money-crazed world we must deal with when we search for work, strive for a paycheck, and covet the latest gadgets at the mall. For a comparison between outer-economy and inner-economy thinking, see the following table.

OUTER-ECONOMY VS. INNER-ECONOMY THINKING

OUTER-ECONOMY (MONEY-CRAZED WORLD) THINKING	INNER-ECONOMY (HEART-AND-SOUL SPACE) THINKING
Others' perceptions come first. What others think takes precedence over my thoughts and feelings.	**My inner voice comes first.** I incorporate my thoughts and feelings into the feedback loop.
The company's bottom line has priority. The organization's financial condition controls my feelings and actions.	**My personal bottom line has priority.** I clarify what I value the most and assess my responses to external conditions.
I heed the job market bellows. I follow job trends as the route to security and happiness.	**I heed my own call.** I trust that my passion and its associated process will lead me forward.
The competition rules. I figure out who my competitors are and what they are doing, and I use my energy to beat them.	**I am my own competition.** I assess my own strengths and then offer quality service based on those strengths.
I have a stock-market-valuation mind-set. I base my self-worth on the daily Dow Jones Industrial Average.	**I have an inner-currency appreciation.** I honor my strengths and persevere to add value by acting on them.

COMING UP FOR AIR

Most of us are genuinely busy as we juggle commuting, working, grocery shopping, exercising, tending to kids, caring for aging parents, and maintaining a home. "I'm busy" has, at least to some degree, become an unthinking way of life. However, it's a condition that blocks reflection—the passageway to personal knowledge and freedom—and intimacy with oneself and others.

Despite my many obligations, I assert my right to reflect on a daily basis. I once told a colleague, "Ideally, I give myself two hours a day for that." She looked at me incredulously, as if to say, "How can you manage that when I'm running nonstop from dawn to dusk?" The fact is, it isn't always easy. Many times, it truly is a struggle. But, what makes me come back to this practice time and again is my belief that reflection is not a waste of time and money. Indeed, reflection is an active inquiry that serves every aspect of my life. As I converse with myself, mull over my thoughts, and write them down, I begin to synthesize and interpret the world around me. I obtain a better understanding of my colleagues and clients and also of my family.

I try to be specific in my musings. I note the ways I might take heightened care when approaching a sensitive matter or how I might give feedback or alter a question to elicit more open or meaningful responses. Without reflection, I'd see myself as a negligent imposter. I'd end up jeopardizing my spirit—compromising myself and my ability to make a difference in other people's lives. For me, reflection is as essential as breathing. It's the process that keeps us grounded by governing our awareness and intention. Reflection serves as the bedrock of every act.

TRYING THE EASY WAY FIRST

If you were to ask me, "What comes easily to you? What is effort-less?" my answer would be that since I was a young boy, I've had a sensitivity to others' needs, an awareness of nuances, and an ability to ask good questions. The questions I ask seem to engage people and evoke both fresh thinking and good decision making. Among the questions I asked myself as a child were, Why are some people kind and others uncaring? Why is it so important for a family to stick together?

Today, I get paid to ask people questions and to help them find a focus for their life. Becky, an executive, traveled internationally and remained on call 24/7 to meet the demands of foreign clients. When she returned to corporate headquarters, she was deluged with meetings, phone calls, and presentations. "Although I love traveling, I can no longer reconcile myself to the time it takes away from the other parts of my life," Becky said. "I also enjoy the intellectual challenge of my job, but I'm feeling really fried. Schlepping bags gets old, and I've given up tennis and music. Now, catching up on sleep is the only thing I care about."

"Becky, do you think a solution is looming on the horizon?" I asked.

"I don't know what else to do but quit," she said.

"What makes you certain that you have to quit?"

"I can't imagine my future, but I don't want it to look or feel like the present."

"When is the last time you took a break?"

"About a year ago. But, I ended up taking care of my sick mom that week."

"You were still on duty, nursing your mother," I noted. "Have you considered taking a vacation, for maybe a month or more, that's especially for you?"

"That's so European!" she said. "I'm not sure my boss would comply, or if I'd get paid."

My concern was that Becky might quit her present job, find a similar job, and replicate the same behavior. Then, we would find ourselves repeating our conversation five years from now. Offering an alternative, I proposed that Becky ask her boss for a six-week leave with pay—a move that would bolster her self-confidence and give her a respite from the daily grind. Becky called me the following week with the news, "My boss has agreed to give me two months off with pay!"

When a client comes to me with a problem, I first try the easy route. We sit down together to consider the client's work-life nuances, anxiety relievers, and vision for the future. Then, we figure out a way to get the client closer to that vision. Often, it boils down to this: First, clarify what you need. Then, ask for it. Sometimes the easy way works.

USING YOUR SPIRITUAL INTELLIGENCE

After being unemployed for several weeks, Vitore took a temporary night job loading freight onto trucks. One evening, a trucker returned to the dock with five pallets of cereal boxes that an overstocked retailer had rejected. With no restock space available, the trucker conferred with the site supervisor and agreed that the cereal could be given to the site employees. However, the general manager stopped the distribution, declaring, "Gifts cannot be taken from independent contractors under any circumstances!" Vitore stood watching as hundreds of cereal boxes were heaved into a crusher.

"What is the significance of this story to you?" I asked.

"I was angry," Vitore said. "My spirit was crushed along with that cereal. That food could have fed the workers and their families."

"Does this story contain a message for you?"

"I need to find a job that will allow me to lead and assert some influence. If I had been the general manager, I would have said, Let's divide the cereal fairly and each take a few boxes home. Without the authority to do what is right, my soul will wither in no time."

"Vitore, what kind of a spirit do you have? I ask a lot of questions, so obviously I have a curious spirit. What about you?"

"I want to be able to make a difference in this world. I guess that makes me not only a caring spirit but a fighting one, too. I want a job that will allow me to advocate for social change."

This kind of self-knowledge is what author Danah Zohar calls *spiritual intelligence:* This type of intelligence functions as the foundation of all other types of intelligence, and it distinguishes humankind from all other creatures. It also acts as the gateway to fully living. "Spiritual intelligence," Zohar says, "is the soul's intelligence. It is the intelligence with which we heal ourselves and with which we make ourselves whole." Our IQ (intelligence quotient) helps us solve rational problems. Our EQ (emotional quotient) helps us assess and develop functional relationships. But, our SQ (spiritual quotient) enlivens the very individual being in each of us. Without it, we'd be crippled and able only to limp through our lives.

Vitore and many of my other clients are smart and emotionally savvy but are still struggling to light that inner flame—or to find a way to nurture it. As the brilliant improvisationalist Robin Williams advised, "You're only given a little spark of madness. You mustn't lose it."

COOKING YOUR OWN WAY

Occasionally, a client begins a session with a story that seems irrelevant to his or her search for more rewarding work. But, I've learned to listen for the story's deeper meaning. For example, Fred, an engineer, told the following anecdote.

————

My son Ebben called and said, "Dad, what are you cooking for dinner?"

I said, "Steak Diane."

"Oh," he said. "Is that the steak that you cook with a mixture of butter, garlic, mustard, half-and-half, and lemon juice?"

"That's the one and, of course, I've doctored the recipe. Tonight, I'm substituting olive oil for butter and adding a bit of pesto."

"Dad," Ebben said, "must you always change the recipe?"

————

As Fred and I reflected on this story, we realized that the way that he cooks mirrors his process at work. As a manager, Fred reads case studies to assess the ways others have solved a particular problem. Then, he devises his own solution by making small changes here and there until he achieves the desired result. I asked Fred, "Why don't you just follow a proven formula?"

"I'm both an analytical and a creative guy," Fred said. "I manage a company in the same way that I cook. If I don't substitute olive oil for butter or throw in a little pesto, I get bored. Adding my own spices keeps me interested and usually sparks other people's interest, as well. Maybe I should have been a chef!"

Winning interviews and advancing your career depend not only on competence but also on expressing your uniqueness. I suggested to Fred that when he gives seminars, he should link his cooking repertoire to his problem-solving ability. A pertinent story can add just the right spice!

Fred's enthusiasm was so contagious that I couldn't help asking myself the question, How do I cook? Here is my personal recipe:

1. Envision what I want to have for dinner—for example, stuffed chicken breast.

2. For ingredients to combine into a stuffing, look in the refrigerator for leftovers and in the pantry for goodies. For example, I might find cheese, walnuts, apricots, rice, and green onions, along with olive oil, pepper, and salt.

3. Believe in my vision and stick with it, despite Amy's quip, Aren't you going to follow a recipe?

4. Combine the ingredients, broil, sprinkle zesty cheese and a dash of lemon on top, and serve.

5. Wait for comments and hopefully compliments!

When I'm cooking, I'm engaged in a miniadventure—trusting my instincts, selecting the best ingredients, and curiously waiting to see how the dish will turn out. I work with my clients in a similar way. First, we establish a vision. What do they want to gain from the Rethinking Work process?

Next, we look for the prime ingredients—passion, beliefs, skills, values, aptitudes, hopes, dreams, and fears—and determine which ones should be added to the mix. Sometimes, it turns out that an ingredient doesn't belong, so we remove it from the next mix. Or, we might add a different ingredient to the mix. At some point along the way, we decide it's time to test the product in the marketplace.

TREASURING YOUR STORIES

Harris Sussman calls himself an unretirement coach. He once began a Harvard lecture by saying, "We are all self-employed." That was fifteen years ago, and I still remember how my heart began to pound as Sussman described the new social contract. I was so inspired that I raced home to put pen to paper, and I began writing a book.

After getting a few chapters down, I invited Sussman to join me for a cup of coffee. He asked why I was so excited about his self-employment philosophy. I answered by telling him a story.

When I was 12, I took a trip with my family to New York City. It was a weekday. All the passengers at the station seemed so serious. I listened for laughter and looked around for a smile. The men all wore dark suits and white shirts. Each held a briefcase in one hand and the *Wall Street Journal* in the other. When the conductor shouted, "Allllll aboard!" they all marched in step and climbed onto the train.

Was this what I had to look forward to? Was I expected to be the same as everyone else? The image haunted me for nearly forty years. These men apparently had a dress code and an unspoken edict from their employers: Produce and we'll guarantee your job; remain loyal and we'll take care of you forever. There's only one catch: You have to give up your individuality.

Fortunately, I grew up in a home where individuality was fostered. My father worked at a big insurance company but didn't join the herd. Instead, he mapped out his strategy and carved out his sales territory. "They never had to manage me," he said. "I set my own goals and saw every day as an opportunity. I ended up earning more than the branch manager!"

My childhood observation of businessmen getting on the train inspired me to consider the ways we relate to work. I now guide people in stepping out of line for the purpose of discovering and con-tributing their unique talents to the world. This story reminds me that being an automaton costs too much; it's better to nurture what is fresh and spontaneous in ourselves.

A few days after our meeting, Sussman sent me the following passage by Albert Camus:

———

I know this, with sure and certain knowledge: A man's work is nothing but this slow trek to rediscover, through the detours of art, those two or three great and simple images in whose presence his heart first opened. This is why, perhaps, after work-ing and producing for twenty years, I still live with the idea that my work has not even begun.

———

FINDING YOUR MOTIVATING STORY

If you've been thinking, "I'm bored with what I do," or, "My job pays the bills but I'm unhappy—work takes too much out of my hide," I encourage you to discover the stories that can free your spirit. Try the following process.

1. Ask yourself, What did I most love to do when I was a child? Or, What is it that sustained me during the happiest period of my life?

2. Write a story about these pleasures. Don't worry about whether the story is good enough.

3. Ask yourself, Which of these pleasures or capacities am I using in my present work?

4. Now, ask yourself, What can I do to increase my pleasure on the job? Focus on one or two behaviors, such as using a particular talent or working with a team.

5. Notice whether your satisfaction and productivity increase as you pay attention to these behaviors.

TACKLING THE MONEY QUESTION

Terry, a public relations expert, earned plenty of money helping his clients look their best when they stepped onto the public stage. The job maintained its allure for several years. But, Terry grew increasingly unhappy with the nature of his work and felt that he was just doing "more of the same." Terry said, "I feel like I'm on a bread-and-water diet. My current income allows me to both meet my alimony payments and live well in my second marriage. But, I'm concerned that if I make a change, I won't have enough money."

"Have you thought about any alternatives?" I asked. "What kind of a change might work for you?"

"Well, yes," Terry said. "I've been attending the same church for years and many of the elders have retired or passed away. A need has surfaced for fresh leadership and a new infrastructure. We need to consider everything from enrollment to fund-raising to accounting and human resource policies, and it's also time to renovate our historic building. I don't know where it might lead, but I can imagine feeling quite fulfilled as a steward, working there part-time to transition out of my current business."

"How much of your time would the church stewardship take?"

"That is the problem," Terry said. "I'd need about fifteen hours a week, which would cut into my billable hours."

"From where I sit, you have a very workable problem. Have you considered how much money is truly enough—in other words, how much you actually need to 'live well'? If your baseline needs require less than the amount you are spending now, you might consider cutting back on your business hours. Then, you'd be able to allocate one-third of your week to church leadership."

Terry said, "The idea of *enough* is so un-American. My friends all want more and more. They never seem to think that they have enough. Most of us never even consider this question."

I asked, "Do you think your friends become happier as they accumulate more?"

Two weeks later, Terry sent me the following note by e-mail:

I left our last session kicking and screaming. I didn't want to give up anything—certainly not money. What kept bugging me, though, was the fact that my current work was costing me plenty. I asked myself the question, What is the price I've been paying to run my PR firm? The answer was, My happiness.

I sat down and performed a "how much is enough" analysis, and I discovered that I could pay myself 20 percent less and still live quite comfortably. So, my wife and I have decided to adjust our expectations, at least for a while. If friends ask us to go with them to a fancy restaurant, I'll be honest about my decision and suggest that we try the local pub!

I returned Terry's e-mail with a quotation from British journalist Holbrook Jackson: Happiness is a form of courage.

—— **Check-In** ——

THE RIGHT
TO REFLECT

After an initial client meeting, I wait a few days for the client's thoughts to settle, and then I check in by e-mail. Usually, I ask a follow-up question that is designed to prod a more thorough process of reflection. This encourages the client to connect the dots—integrating his or her past with the present by culling the ideas, feelings, strengths, and experiences that are relevant to the current search. Similarly, I encourage you to complete the exercises that have appeared in this chapter and to then check in here before you go on to the next chapter. It is my belief that you can benefit greatly by doing so.

Here are the check-in questions for you to answer:

- What is the most stifling thing about your work? Thoroughly describe it.

- What qualities do you now value most?

- Are you growing? If so, how?

- Who in your life might support your continued growth?

- How much money is enough for you?

THE PERMISSION TO EXPLORE

WHAT WORK ENERGIZES YOUR SPIRIT?

Live the questions now. Perhaps you will then gradually,
without noticing it, live along some distant day into the answer.
RAINER MARIA RILKE

A colleague tells you about a great job in his firm that offers super pay. But, you don't just go for the bait. You stop and give yourself permission to explore the situation: What is the job going to ask of me? And, you rate your personal interest in the job: To what degree am I truly passionate about this position? How do the daily job responsibilities relate to my skills and talents? How will I be of the most help to others? Will I learn anything new from this type of work?

The biggest mistake we tend to make during our quest for truer work is jumping in—without allowing ourselves the time to look

THE RETHINKING WORK® PROCESS

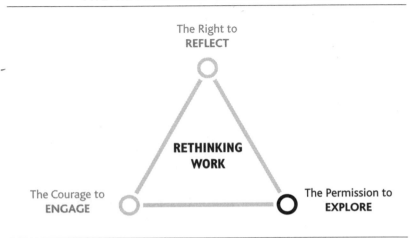

The Right to
REFLECT

**RETHINKING
WORK**

The Courage to
ENGAGE

The Permission to
EXPLORE

around and view a situation from all sides. We assess a job, prematurely, by looking through the narrow lens of responsibilities versus compensation and employee benefits. We operate according to some external chart that says, Your next job should be *x* and the salary *y*. By doing this, however, we're playing it safe; we never get to explore new territory, travel beyond our present job definition, or venture into any unknown.

Ferdinand Magellan learned much about ships and navigation while working as a royal messenger for Portugal, but he dreamt, not of continuing in his role, but of circumnavigating the world. When his project was rejected by the king of Portugal, he petitioned the king of Spain. I encourage you to adopt Magellan's spirit and begin an exploration to find out both what matters most to you and who is most likely to support your dream.

HEEDING THE CALL TO EXPLORE

My clients cite a variety of reasons for wanting to change jobs, but in the long run, the reasons all boil down to wanting to feel more alive and engaged with their work. Here are some of their complaints:

- "I was earning a paycheck, but that, in and of itself, doesn't add enough value to my life. I left to explore alternatives because I felt 'blah.'"

- "I'm comfortable but miserable. I feel I have no choice but to question what I really want."

- "Keeping score—acquiring a bigger house and a fancier car— is no longer my game. Life is wheeling on, and I refuse to get run over."

- "Work has been like a methadone clinic. We all stay because we're waiting for our six-month bonuses. After receiving them, we just return to the same old junk. Where is the joy in it? I'm ending my fix right now."

- "It feels like we're all just interchangeable parts—so many people leave this place each week. I keep waiting for my number to come up."

What have you been saying to yourself or to your friends? What is motivating you to strike out and explore some new terrain?

If you're overidentified with one company and tired of the routine, or if your company is downsizing and you see your job creeping toward extinction, then you're a prime candidate for the Rethinking Work process. View your situation as a call to exploration. It's no longer about the company and its needs; it's about your skills and talents and your needs. Don't waste time on self-recrimination. Remember that change is a natural part of life.

GETTING PAST THE FEELING OF ROUTINE

Even work you love can become routine. You may have trained diligently to develop a new skill, but the time has come when you feel a twinge of complacency. Your tasks now feel predictable and you've begun to fidget. You may blame this discomfort on the pressures of the job, your impossible boss, a string of demanding customers, or the stress of your commute.

I challenge you to stop looking outward for the cause. Instead of asking, "How can I change my boss and my co-workers?" ask yourself, "What am I missing in my work? What do I need to feel invigorated?" You work your way out of the doldrums by connecting with the skills and talents that make you come alive. Rather than seeking new employment right away, make up your mind to explore your inner economy—to probe your beliefs, experiences, and past behavior—to find out what it is that cooled your enthusiasm and left you feeling disconnected and out of sorts.

When I feel I've lost my edge, it's generally because I've ignored my creativity or stopped digging for new ways to help my clients find their magic. Lately, writing has become my tool for reinvigoration. Every day, I spend a couple of hours questioning my main assumptions and experimenting with words. Writing allows me to examine my experiences and find new ways to challenge my clients to examine theirs. When I was halfway through writing this book, I said to Amy, "My practice has never been better, and I think it's because my pen has clarified and energized my focus." At the end of this chapter,

I've provided some structured writing exercises that I hope will do the same for you.

RECOGNIZING THAT YOU'RE A WORK IN PROGRESS

Whereas writing can help you know yourself better, a good friend can boost your confidence and help you through a period of uncertainty. Changing your work—or any portion of your life—means leaving the old maps behind and striking out for unknown territory. The road will always be easier when you share it with a friend.

My best friend, Vin, and I upheld a tradition of running together every Saturday morning, no matter what the weather. One of our favorite spots was an inviting, wooded path in Concord, Massachusetts. The setting was picturesque, and the run became the highlight of my week. The obvious draw was staying in shape, yet on those days I also felt treasured by another human being—not for what I might become, but for who I was, exactly, in the present moment.

Together, we explored the mysteries of life. Coming up with the "right" answers wasn't important; it was the process that engaged us. When is the best time to remarry? How will I know when I've found the right person? Am I doing the right work? Should I change jobs now, or wait? What's it like to be responsible for a child? Should my job remain stable if other areas of my life are in flux? No matter what subject arose, we didn't need to please or agree with one another. Instead, we ran down unknown trails, wondering and exchanging ideas. When either of us thought he had an answer, the other would tease him by saying, "Perfect!" Of course, we knew that life is a work in progress and that there is no such thing as a perfect answer.

Leave the sublime to the fleeting moment, because it isn't something you can control. Our lives are full of strains, stresses, and ambiguities. To draw in fresh opportunities, you need to stifle your ideas of perfection and respect the natural rhythms of trial-and-error exploration.

Binh, a financial analyst, learned this lesson. When we first met, he said, "I've been thinking about changing jobs, and I finally found an opening for a position I really want. I received an offer from a bank to work as a financial planner. The catch is that the work is all commission-based. Although I'd love to advise people and help them structure their finances, the situation isn't perfect. I'm afraid that, in the beginning, I won't make any money."

"You've searched for quite a while, it appears, without uncovering the perfect scenario," I said.

"I could remain in my comfort zone and earn a regular salary from a job that doesn't honor my passion," he confessed. "But, now I'm in a fix. I want to follow my North Star, but I don't want to be stuck without a paycheck. The upside of the new position is that if I succeed at it, I will be doing work I really love and earning well beyond my current salary."

"I'm not sure you're really in such a fix," I offered. "Flaws will appear in any path you might choose. Why not explore the compensation issue further? I've worked with others who received some combination of salary and commission. You might investigate other banks and financial institutions that could offer similar jobs with different pay structures."

"You know, as you were talking, I was thinking that if I took the new position and it didn't pan out, I could work as an analyst again while I regrouped." Binh was grasping the idea that it might not come down to an all-or-nothing scenario. He could reach his goals through a process of exploration and experimentation.

"That fallback position will act as your parachute," I said. "When you put yourself in auspicious situations, your belief and your passion can carry you to levels beyond your imagination. In the process, you'll unleash your spirit—and things will take off so fast that you won't even look back."

Binh really liked that notion. "This is the most challenging work decision I've had to make yet, but I believe I'll make a very good 'money doctor.' I also know that staying put would mean lying to myself. In the past, I've made decisions that seemed irrational on the outside, but somehow I felt at peace with them, and things worked out fine in the end."

LOOKING FOR UNEXPECTED OPENINGS

No one reading this book should feel that freeing one's spirit and earning enough money are mutually excusive. If you are willing and able to confront your fears about stepping out of line, you can end up having both.

I make it a point to remember the times I managed to overcome my fears. For example, once in the early 1970s, I was vacationing in Big Sur, California, where a series of mudslides had destroyed the roads and washed out many of the hiking trails. I still wanted to explore the Pacific coast's natural beauty, so I started walking along a narrow path, which led into a cave. I was apprehensive, but I pressed on, and soon the darkness opened into a panorama, revealing pounding surf below and a big blue sky above. It was trusting my gut—not knowing the complete picture or what might lie in store—that led me to that opening.

I deeply believe that having the courage to follow one's instincts is what makes a good explorer. This trait has served me well in my career. It has taught me to listen to myself and advance toward opportunities.

For a committed explorer, this process is never ending. Kimberly, the former director of diversity for a high-technology manufacturing company, had much to say about the importance of showing one's true colors. "There was a time in my life," she said, "when I realized that I had gone gray. I felt gray. I wore gray. It seemed as though I was fading away. As I departed the office one evening, feeling tired from the stresses of the corporate world, I saw my reflection in a hallway window and had an epiphany. I realized that I had dampened my spirit in the workplace—and that I needed to change that reality. So, I donated my gray suits to charity, and I began making a conscious effort to show the people at work who I was. I wonder how many of us who work for large organizations lose our identity on the job?"

Kimberly reinvigorated herself by spending her winters in Florida and her summers on Cape Cod. She now works as a consultant, running a mobile business that serves clients throughout the United States, while also creating diversity and productivity programs for companies that offer their workers the same kind of freedom.

LEARNING THE TWELVE RULES FOR EXPLORERS

As an explorer, you won't travel a set route from point A to point Z. A lot of zigzagging will occur as you run into the unknown. Sometimes, you will clearly see your route. At other times, you'll feel hopelessly adrift. This is all part of the journey you'll be taking. Along the way, however, you can make yourself more comfortable by abiding by twelve rules:

- Expect discomfort.

- Get support.

- Reclaim your innocence.

- Come to terms with your relationship to money.

- Dare to ask new questions.

- Clarify your direction.

- Recycle your skills and interests.

- Listen to others but assign the most weight to your inner voice.

- Take a class.

- Donate your time.

- Find new ways to connect with your client base.

- Remember the recipe for success.

The following sections describe these rules in detail.

Expecting Discomfort

Distress is a sign, not necessarily that something has gone terribly wrong, but that something is in the process of changing. During any transition, a person commonly feels anxious—both threatened and excited about new possibilities. Randall, for example, was leaving a large corporation to join two partners in a start-up venture. "I've become accustomed to perks, promotions, and paychecks, so my apprehension kicks in when I think about leaving," he said. "However, I have never felt more alive than in the past five years."

Getting Support

Find one or more fellow travelers. Share your goals and concerns with others who are exploring new ways of being in the world. Listen to their experiences. Learn from and support each other. In this phase of the Rethinking Work process, collaboration is essential.

Reclaiming Your Innocence

Exploring is a childlike (not childish) behavior requiring that you remain open to new experiences. When Gabriella was barely 3, we played daily in the park. She would throw stones into the pond, experimenting with the sounds they made, and she would flip rocks over, searching for crawly things. One day Gabriella pointed to a silver object in the sky. I hadn't realized until that moment that the town was situated along an air transit route. I wondered what else I'd been missing. The next day I said to Gabriella, "Let's go out and explore to see whether we can find anything new."

When one of my clients enters this phase of the Rethinking Work process, I recommend that he or she allot at least one hour a week to explore a new section of the neighborhood. It's important to cultivate a sense of openness and to explore one's physical surroundings. If you try this exercise, you may be surprised to see how many things you've failed to notice before—things that you like or dislike or that amuse or surprise you. I call this exercise "The Eye Opener" because it helps activate your sense of wonder and discovery.

Coming to Terms with Your Relationship to Money

While participating in one of my seminars for Boston College alumni, Sahira said, "I'm making enough money now but find little meaning in my work. My biggest fear is that if I go for the meaning, I won't make enough." I turned to the audience and asked, "Would you raise your hand if you feel the same concern?" Most of the hands went up. So, over the next two hours, we explored the question, "How do we generate both meaning and money?"

Sahira decided to test her vision of the combination in her current position as an engineer for an innovative software company. She worked on team building by encouraging her colleagues to collaborate with one another and share their ideas as opposed to maintaining the tunnel vision that had been causing each of them to focus on external goals. She knew that cultivating the group's trust and patience would take time, but she felt that openly sharing ideas and opinions would stimulate morale, make the company a more enjoyable place to work, and enhance the bottom line.

What Sahira didn't account for was this: With more ideas on the table, the team members clamored for more recognition. She met this challenge by naming each one a coauthor of the software that was being developed. The software eventually proved successful and was sold to multiple corporate clients. Within a year, Sahira was scooped up by another company and given the title of vice president—along with a bigger salary.

Daring to Ask New Questions

After receiving his performance review, Smitty didn't ask his boss, Mitch, what he could do to improve his department's performance. This time, he asked instead what he needed to do to become a vice president. Mitch muttered the usual line about first needing to grow the sales intake. So, Smitty asked, "Can we explore the fiscal condition of the company?" He then presented a few ideas about how to increase profitability. Mitch scheduled another meeting with the vice president of human resources to discuss the possibility of offering Smitty a more senior position.

Clarifying Your Direction

Rona fell into sales because she excelled at developing relationships, solving problems, and closing deals, but she felt underutilized. "I want to find something that fits my personality better," she said. After a period of reflection, Rona felt confident about the core skills she wanted to use: questioning, interviewing, strategizing, and problem solving. We determined that these skills were portable and that she might explore the world of consulting. Between the two of us, we knew seven consultants, and Rona contacted each one to ask,

- What do you do on a daily basis?

- What route did you take to get into this profession?

- What do you like about your work? How does it fit your personality?

- If you could change one thing about your work, what would it be?

- What recommendations would you make to someone who wanted to start a career in consulting?

Rona's investigation provided a wealth of information that helped her evaluate not only the market for this kind of work and the type of person who is happy in it but also how she might use her talents and fulfill her own desires.

Although exploration takes planning and commitment, it's not as time consuming in the end as accepting the wrong job and then starting your quest all over again.

Recycling Your Skills and Interests

I began my career as a special education teacher focusing on task analysis. Rather than assume that every student could learn to tie a shoelace in three steps, I would break down the task into as many components as necessary to foster confidence in a particular child and to help him or her successfully tie a bow. In my current practice, I do the same thing on a larger scale. I help my clients break down the process of reinventing their work so that each of them can proceed not only with a can-do attitude but with enough information to bolster his or her chance of success.

Look back over the different jobs you've had and list those moments that gave you particular joy or satisfaction. What skills were you using then? How might they be revived?

Listening to Others but Assigning the Most Weight to Your Inner Voice

Bosses and colleagues may not encourage you to explore new territory simply because they are struggling with their own constraints. "I examined many options, and decided to sell my business to seed research and the possibility of a start-up," said Samuel. "Most of my friends thought my choice was risky—even crazy—and I was tempted to agree with them. But, I've done my homework. I trust myself, and I feel privileged to have a dream."

Taking a Class

Don't rashly quit your day job or blindly take the next promotion. Instead, seek out new alternatives. Test the waters by signing up for a course that builds your knowledge of a particular field or craft. Hillary, the director of outreach for a small nonprofit organization, enrolled in a seminar her boss recommended to help her determine whether she had the skills and temperament necessary to become a leader. "I came away from that experience feeling confident that I could handle such a job," she said, "but somewhat ambivalent about the time commitment involved." Hillary decided to remain in her current position while searching for a similar one that would offer more pay and flexibility.

Donating Your Time

To investigate your options and hone in on your focus, volunteer your talent. One of my clients, a budding photographer, offered his services, pro bono, to schools, amateur theater groups, and charitable organizations as a way of getting started. Doing so connected him to his customers and contributed to his self-confidence. After his first shoot, he said, "Now, I'm a professional photographer!"

Finding New Ways to Connect with Your Client Base

Lindsey had worked for a large architectural firm for years but was determined to hang out her own shingle. To prepare for the big day, she crafted a business plan and set up a home office. After approaching her first potential client, she sent me the following note:

_____

I was completely unsuccessful in selling my service. I realize now that I should have taken a different approach. Instead of talking about myself, I should have asked about the client. In the future, I plan on asking questions about the client's passions and lifestyle and then shaping my responses to fit the story I hear.

_____

Remembering the Recipe for Success

The recipe for success contains two steps:

1. Do your homework.

2. Apply the lessons you've learned to the outside world.

Your ABCs for Rethinking Work

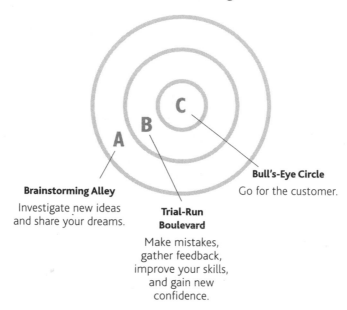

Brainstorming Alley

Investigate new ideas
and share your dreams.

**Trial-Run
Boulevard**

Make mistakes,
gather feedback,
improve your skills,
and gain new
confidence.

Bull's-Eye Circle

Go for the customer.

Often, I use a simple diagram to describe the Rethinking Work process (see the figure above). I draw a target made up of three concentric circles and tell my client, "Start in the A zone by discovering what kind of work speaks to your spirit. Keep exploring in the B zone as you test your new assumptions. Leave yourself plenty of room to experiment here. Remember that it's okay to rethink your course and change direction. In the B zone you'll begin to learn about your audience. You'll rehearse your presentation with your friends and colleagues. You'll get valuable feedback and hone your vision—all at no cost. By the time you get to the C zone, you'll have done your homework and be ready to go for the bull's-eye!"

FEARING THE LOSS OF INTEREST IN ANY JOB

One of the most common fears I encounter is the apprehension that a new job will soon become as boring as the last. While raising a family, Shema taught mathematics in the middle schools, counseled teenage girls, and worked as a pastry chef. But, none of these jobs lasted longer than two years. "I have enjoyed each position, but the trouble is, I'm easily bored," Shema said. "I'm afraid I'll continue in this cycle of running from one thing to the next, wasting time and money as I try new things. I may even end up losing my husband's emotional support."

I asked, "What criteria have driven your work choices?"

"A desire for independence and a wish to make a difference in people's lives. I'm a healing, helping advocate. Counseling, teaching, and tutoring seemed to fit. In those fields, I also had a flexible schedule, so I could get home for my kids at 3:00 as well as cook the evening meal."

"So, why did you become a pastry chef?"

"I was feeling fatigued from all my family responsibilities. I was on call 24/7 at home, and my work at the schools and the Teen Learning Center was demanding. I needed to retreat for a while. When I was growing up, my parents owned a bakery. After school and on Saturdays, my brother and I worked as my father's helpers by making and selling apple and cherry strudel, Viennese crescents, and our signature pastry, Hungarian cream cake. When I took the job making pastries at an upscale restaurant, no training was required. My hours were short, and I could focus on the food, and not on people, for a change."

"Which restaurant? I'd like to sample one of your desserts!"

"Sorry, but you can't. After four months, I could no longer stand the isolation, so I quit. I missed the interaction with people and the intellectual challenge of my previous work. I still love working with kids, but I don't want to go back into a school system."

"To gain a fresh perspective, why not give yourself a break from the job search? Take some time to clear your head and rest your body."

"Stop my frenetic pace? Ha! I'm sure you're right. But, if I do, will the outcome be any different? I haven't found any type of work that I can stick with yet."

"Before you judge yourself too harshly, let's explore a little further. I've been working with another client, Marissa, who sounded very much like you at first. She was the CEO of a nonprofit organization and a mother of two who described herself as bored, stuck, and fearful. Keep in mind that it's absolutely normal for us to tire from our stations or the goals we've achieved. At one point, Marissa said, 'I imagine myself at work sucking on a straw and trying to get the last drop of liquid from the cup. However, nothing remains but air, so all I do is slurp.' Marissa and I concluded that a traditional job hunt would perpetuate that awful feeling. Instead, we reframed her quest as a search for meaning."

"You mean, a 'cause search' instead of a job search?" Shema asked.

"Exactly. For years, Marissa had spearheaded health care reform in major metropolitan areas. She worked nonstop—managing, fundraising, and organizing because she believed in the greater mission. Every time she changed jobs, she found a cause that deeply resonated with her beliefs, and she then signed on for whatever needed to be accomplished. By the time she came to me, she was burned out and thought the answer was to hide out in a humdrum job. But, that solution didn't work. She needed to engage her heart again."

Suddenly, Shema said, "You know, I can't stand SUVs! They do nothing but ruin the environment, not to mention the fact that they hog the road. The environment is a cause I could really get behind."

"Okay, you're enthused; but, before you step on the accelerator, you still need to take a rest. After a break of four to six weeks, you can start your cause search. You might begin by calling the Massachusetts Department of Environmental Protection. Ask about its current priorities. Or, run an Internet search for organizations that support a green environment and choose two or three to investigate thoroughly. If they continue to hold your interest, meet with people in each organization to deepen your understanding of its culture and how it functions. Then, step back and assess whether your values, skills, background, and lifestyle match the organization's mission. You may want to ask a friend to be your sounding board. We can then evaluate the situation to decide on next steps, including the possibility that you might need to expand your inquiry—or even find another cause. Along the way, you can feel free to check in with me."

"I like it," Shema said. "I'm not going to get dragged into the 'Oh, please hire me' syndrome. Instead, I'm going do my cause research and begin the matching process. I might look into global warming and chemical exposure. Our friend's daughter became ill after they moved into a new house. The freshly planted shrubs were browning and the soil was retaining water. Engineers discovered toxins and concluded that the soil was tainted. I think I've got enough to chew on now."

"That's the idea, explore to widen your horizons. I can help you focus on your prospects later."

"Cliff, you don't happen to drive an SUV?"

FINDING YOUR PASSION

Leslie, an account executive for a technology communications firm, had trouble deciding which job market to explore. "My clients, mostly nonprofit organizations, are all politically active," she said. "One focuses on cleaning up inland lakes and streams and invited me to spend my vacation fishing at one of its clean sites. I went and I gagged. I am just not passionate about that cause, and besides, I can't stand touching fish. I don't think I can network there."

"Any cause or business can feel slimy if it doesn't align with your passion," I suggested. "How about converting the word *cause* to *interest*. An interest can energize you, whereas a cause can run its course. It's better to admit, rather than judge, your preferences."

"Well, the truth is, I'm a fanatic about sports cars. I drive a Porsche—an older 911 model. I also test performance clothing, such as lightweight, breathable jackets and perforated triathlon sneakers, for an inventor/engineer who operates a university lab."

"So, let's explore a bit and see what things excite your passion."

Leslie had started out looking at causes she thought she could get behind. I asked her to make a list of her interests so we could compare the two approaches. Here is what she presented during our first interview:

Causes	Interests
Hunger relief	Sports cars
Clean air	Performance clothing
Solar energy	Open-source software
AIDS research	Eastern wellness systems
Planned peace	Travel and vacation planning

I began by asking, "How do you feel about hunger relief?"

"I care," Leslie said, "but I'm not excited."

"How do you feel about clean air?"

"I love it, of course, but it's better left to the scientists and the environmentalists."

Leslie showed the same willingness to delegate when it came to solar energy, AIDS research, and planned peace.

When we got to the list of interests, however, she glowed—especially when we discussed athletic clothing. With her background in client management, she could network with running-equipment manufacturers and designers and explore branding and marketing roles. Leslie would investigate not only potential job fit but also organizational culture. She was looking for professional camaraderie, an upbeat team with a sense of humor, and respect for individual contributions.

To find out whether a company met her criteria, Leslie decided to ask each of her interviewees,

- What do you like about working here?

- Can you describe your work environment?

- What is valued the most at this company? How do you know?

- What happens when you disagree with your boss and air your differences?

- Can you tell me a story that demonstrates how you work?

The last question was vital because it's so open ended and unstructured. Leslie wasn't going to ask, "Can you tell me a story that demonstrates how you work collaboratively?" The idea was to see what associations cropped up for the person being interviewed rather than imposing Leslie's criteria or needs.

SEEING INFORMATION
AS THE WINNING EDGE

At this point in your exploration, you might wonder, "Why would anyone want to talk with me? I'm looking for information, not a specific job. Won't people think it's weird if I call them up to pick their brain?"

If a few people refuse to give you an hour of their time, don't worry. Perhaps your approach needs a little tweaking. Or, maybe they really are too busy. Just don't let any of these reasons stop you from making the next call. Onward, as I say to my clients. Plenty of people would relish sharing their experiences, learning something about you, and hearing your report on "what it's like out there in the marketplace." When you engage others in a confident manner, you give the impression that you have a finger on the pulse of the marketplace. You can validate their feelings that these are challenging times calling for creative thinking—and such validation may help them on their journey, too.

According to Charles Handy, author of the groundbreaking *Age of Unreason* (Harvard Business School Press, 1989), "We change by exploration not by retracing well-known paths."

TURNING ON YOUR SPIGOT

"Dry" is the way Lateefah, a 52-year-old health care manager, described her work to me. "My spigot has been turned off. I've been surviving by dripping—doing just enough to keep my boss happy and to pay the bills."

Lateefah began her career as a social worker and moved into inner-city community building. She facilitated town meetings and group get-togethers that gave the stakeholders—politicians, police officers, school system personnel, and members of other special interest groups—a platform to both air their differences and work for after-school programs, better housing and education, and safer streets. The work was exciting for five or six years, but at the same time that the funding flattened out, Lateefah started a new family. Her need for regular hours and higher pay brought her to a job in community relations at a large hospital.

Although Lateefah received an unexpected promotion to a management position, she felt that something was missing. She said, "I need a mission that is heartfelt and that includes direct contact with the members of my community. Although mortgage payments knock monthly and tuition payments will arrive soon, focusing primarily on money is a killer—it's a goal that hasn't panned out for me yet."

Considering Lateefah's desire to both improve people's lives and increase her income, we explored some new areas, such as corporate training, employee relations, and outplacement and career counseling.

Several months later, she was laid off with only one month's severance pay.

"Do you have a plan to keep yourself afloat financially after your severance runs out?" I asked.

"Abandoning my search is out of the question," she said. "Fortunately, one of the outplacement firms offered me a contract that involves helping to downsize a client company. Although I can't say the work thrills me, I've got some interest and plenty of experience in helping people get back on their feet. It's also a way to earn enough money while I continue to rethink my work.

"The ability to listen to others is such a gift," I said. "And, you listen so well. As I'm sure you know, people become anxious after losing their job, and some of them panic. Yes, I think you can help these people harness their feelings and reframe their skills while continuing to do the same for yourself."

"One new area has begun to pique my interest. While I was networking, I met a biotech manager who facilitates employee leadership groups. I saw the group members raising questions regarding their projects and then hearing solutions from others. I thought, 'Wow, these people look as though they're having a blast while improving the business at the same time.'"

"Did this manager remind you at all of yourself from your community-building days?"

"Why, yes, he did. Like me, he raised many good questions, encouraged participation from the group members, and rarely offered his own opinion. He elicited the collective genius from the group process. But, I'm not sure if community building would suit me now."

"Wait just a minute. I think you have found your own solution. Did you just hear yourself say 'collective genius?'"

Lateefah's face flushed and her eyes widened.

I asked, "What does 'collective genius' mean?"

"It means something like the practice of building collaboration among stakeholders by raising questions and encouraging debate. It also means sharing problems as well as solutions to increase productivity and morale."

"Great, so, how about going back to interview that biotech manager? Find out more about how he fosters collective genius. His company is investing in this process for a reason. Ask him, too, whether he received any special training for this type of facilitation."

A few days later, I sent Lateefah the following note:

————————

The idea of "collective genius" seems to have turned your drip into a flow. You might further investigate how this notion could be useful to others. Try performing an Internet search for terms such as *executive attrition, leadership turnover,* and *Fortune 500 management revolving door.* Try broadening your perspective so you can substantiate a marketplace need for your abilities. Good luck in establishing the "outplacement" anchor. It will provide a foundation from which to explore the idea of collective genius. Keep me posted on your progress.

————————

Lateefah responded,

————————

My hunch is that the pace of executive resignations has increased for reasons ranging from scandals to retirement to poor performance. There's a gap to be filled—filled by encouraging leadership activity to percolate in other divisions of organizations. Thank you for listening to, understanding, and supporting me. I'm grateful to be on this course."

————————

WHEN THE PROCESS DOESN'T HAPPEN FAST ENOUGH

As the crocuses bloomed this spring, I contemplated all the outdoor tasks on my agenda: raking and seeding the lawn, edging and mulching the flowerbeds, cleaning the drainpipes, patching the cement walkway, and painting the trim on the north side of the house. I naively expected to complete this overhaul over the next few weeks. I planned to start that Saturday morning by scraping the wood and painting the trim, but it turned out that nature wasn't so accommodating. It rained the whole day. "Darn, I lost this weekend, and the next two have already been earmarked for other tasks."

I have since learned that attempting to control reality is a waste of time. Instead, I redirect my energy when I feel thwarted by a given task. No way to paint the trim? Now, I find an indoor chore to tackle, and I take great pleasure in crossing it off my list.

The same dynamic applies when my clients explore the marketplace. First, they generate contact lists and start their informational interviews. At that point, they expect lightbulbs to go on and illuminate their options. Of course, the process doesn't usually happen so quickly, and, in the meantime, my clients must learn how to redirect and reinvest their precious energy.

Wallace was in his mid-50s and had worked for twenty-seven years as a trainer, manager, and consultant. After losing his last position in the wake of an organizational merger, he decided to rethink his strategy. His next step was to network with people in corporations, consulting firms, and nonprofit organizations to take the pulse of the marketplace and find out which direction would be the most suitable for him to pursue.

After three months, I asked Wallace, "How many networking interviews have you had so far?"

He replied, "Seventy-five. I've contacted everyone I know and then some, but I'm discouraged. By now, I thought I'd be clear about my direction. Secretly, I even hoped I'd have landed a job or at least a consulting gig."

"Can we put your discouragement aside for a moment and discuss what you learned from your exploration?"

"Several things. First, the market for training and development is diverse and competitive, especially at the top. Second, I'm not as interested in training as in building leadership. Third, age discrimination lurks in corporate hallways. I'm 56, and the younger faces seemed to turn away from me. One vice president was young enough to be one of my sons. Last, I've come to see that no one is really going to hire me but me."

"What do you mean?"

"Well, you've been saying that rethinking work is all about creating my future. My networking has delivered this very message in spades: It's up to me to find my focus. Everyone else is too preoccupied with their own goals to attend to mine."

"That's fair to say, but let's not rule out reciprocity. As you begin to find your niche, the marketplace will respond. In the meantime, let's discuss some methods that will allow you to harness all your energy."

Wallace and I identified the top five contacts from his network. He sensed that these people were genuinely interested in his expertise in leadership development.

"The idea of calling them again is scary," Wallace said. "What if I don't get a job or even any bites?"

"At least you will deepen your relationships. Ask each person a set of questions that moves from general to specific: What are your current overall business priorities? What is your training and development staff doing to support managers and executives? What particular interventions are working? What areas may need shoring up? Given what you know about my background, do you see a potential match for part-time consulting or, possibly, a full-time position?"

"I see," Wallace said. "These questions will help me manage my anxiety and also find out what's going on inside the company."

"That's right. As you probe, you'll not only appear more confident, but you'll gain the opportunity to demonstrate your expertise while deepening your knowledge of the company's needs."

"What if, in the end, we come to a dead zone after exploring all these questions?"

"Just pause, take a deep breath, and ask another question, such as 'Where do you think we are now in our process?' or, 'Do you have any recommendations for me at this point?' If you feel that synergy is taking place, ask instead, 'It seems that there may be a need for my expertise in coaching one of your directors. Could we talk specifically about this project?'"

As Wallace began to understand how to recognize and manage his tension, he was able to convert it into usable energy.

PERFORMING THE "HOW DO I ADD VALUE TO YOUR LIFE?" EXERCISE

At this point in the process, I give my clients an assignment to build their courage and self-confidence. The assignment goes like this: Ask six to eight people—friends, colleagues, and family members—the question, "How do I add value to your life?" The intent of this exercise is to provide you with a snapshot of yourself and your most valued attributes. Right now, you may be worried about your negative qualities and be asking yourself, Why would anybody want to hire me? Our goal is to discover the many skills and qualities for which you are appreciated. Often, this exercise highlights character traits that you normally take for granted. Many of the comments you receive will be eye-openers, underscoring talents that may prove useful in your search for more meaningful work.

A word of advice, though: Don't rush the exercise. Allow yourself two to four weeks to identify the people you wish to contact. Then, send a note, such as the following one, that explains the process to each person:

How do I add value to your life?

As you probably know, I am working with Cliff Hakim, a career consultant who is helping me find more meaningful work.

My task this week is to ask a handful of people I trust to tell me how I add value to their lives. I have chosen you because your insights mean a great deal to me. Just a paragraph or a couple of bullet points will do.

Cliff asked for a seven-day turnaround (e-mail is fine). If you're too busy to tackle this right now, let me know and I'll find somebody else. In the meantime, thanks for supporting my journey.

My clients forward the responses to me, and I look for general themes. Although the clients are typically anxious for my interpretations, I ask to hear their perspectives first. Here's a note that my client, Rachael, received from her friend Leonora:

Rachael, you take me very seriously. You make me feel attended to. You always check in and ask about my activities as well as my moods and feelings. This intensity of interaction is

unusual. Your attention provides more than support, camaraderie, and inspiration. I feel safety in knowing that you would
never accept a response of "All is fine" from me. You would see
through that if I were in trouble. I am certain that you would
see me falling no matter how hard I might try to hide it. I imagine myself always depending on you to provide this degree
of authenticity in our relationship, for which I am extremely
grateful.

———————

"It's hard taking in all this wonderful feedback," Rachael said.
"After reading all the other notes as well, I wonder if it's really me
that the others are talking about."

Rachael is in the throes of accepting her natural talents—her
abilities to listen and make others feel secure. Natural talents are our
genetic aptitudes, analogous to the color of our eyes. Yet, often they
are buried beneath the roles we play at work. A series of "shoulds"
and "oughts" can sabotage our heart's desire—weakening and sometimes compromising all our efforts. Rachael's confidants described
several of her natural gifts: curiosity, enthusiasm, a sense of humor,
intellectual firepower, open-mindedness, and a flair for multitasking.
I encouraged Rachael to use these treasures in her exploration
process. "These talents are precious currency. They will help you
make a wise career investment."

RAISING THE BAR ON TAKING RISKS

At the core of exploring is risk taking, and regardless of our personal tolerance for it, the bar is constantly rising. The volatility of the

economy and the transformation of the business world require us to change and grow. Mia, a landscaper, was contemplating a new career. When we spoke about facing the unknown, she felt inspired by her experience as a mountain climber. "We awoke at 4:00 a.m. after hardly sleeping to begin the arduous trek up a 15,000-foot mountain pass. I had Achilles tendonitis, and my friend was having lots of trouble with the altitude, but we persevered. When we arrived, all our fatigue and pain disappeared with the joy of reaching the top and looking down across the miles of mountains and valleys around us."

I asked, "How is this mountain climbing story connected to your career exploration?"

"When I climb, I need to let go of my fear and get on with the trek. It doesn't matter whether I'm in Nepal or here in Boston. I figure this is the moment to go and see what's up the mountain or around the bend."

Goethe, the great German poet and philosopher, said, "The dangers of life are infinite, and among them is safety." Most people who are dissatisfied with their career are feeling bored and stuck because they've somehow played it safe. So, with Goethe's philosophy in mind, I ask, "What precipice awaits you? What is your challenge today?"

The next chapter, "The Courage to Engage," focuses on what you need to do to land on solid ground.

—— **Check-In** ——

THE PERMISSION TO EXPLORE

Remember that your creativity is the means to a greater vision—that of connecting the dots in your life—and to taking action. The following questions will help you clarify your thoughts and thus stimulate your creativity.

- What questions do you need to ask yourself and others before you take your next job, advance in your company, or start a new business?

- What makes you come alive? What would make you hum at work?

- What fears or obstacles stand in your way?

- Might you overcome your fear by taking a step to the side or even a step back? Can you name that step?

- Where could you volunteer your time as a way to explore an interest and contribute to a worthy cause?

- Have you explored enough for now? Is it time to push off? How do you know it's time to move forward?

THE COURAGE TO ENGAGE

HOW CAN YOU MAKE YOUR IDEAL REAL?

You can steer yourself any direction you choose.
DR. SEUSS, *OH, THE PLACES YOU'LL GO!*

By now, you've asked yourself the two most important questions: What excites me the most? and, How do I make the best use of my skills and talents? Let's consider how you can step out and engage the world. During this stage, you'll want to be able to answer these questions: How do I make my mission clear to others? How do I sell my product or develop my market? What is the best way to keep up my momentum? When is it time to seek a partner or hire additional staff?

The most important thing I can tell you at this point is this: Whenever you feel unsure, return to the tools outlined in the preceding chapters of this book. Remember that this is a journey for which *you* set the pace.

THE RETHINKING WORK® PROCESS

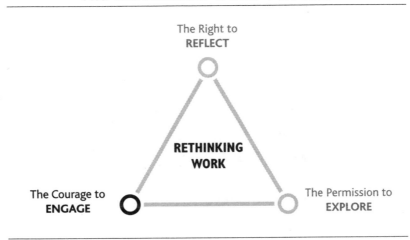

Consider what happens during the biological process of life. Our lungs expel carbon dioxide, a waste substance, while our red blood cells carry oxygen to our beating heart and eventually feed all our other organs. Each organ has a unique purpose, but it is all of the organs working together that enables us to function. Similarly, all the Rethinking Work stages together enable us to function during our journey. In other words, we continue to *reflect* and *explore* as we set forth to *engage* the world.

Each stage has its distinct role but also has permeable boundaries, giving us the option of reassessing and regrouping at any crucial moment. When you're stuck regarding who you are or what you want, use the tools of reflection. When you're confused about your values, your direction, or the kind of place you want to work in, use the tools of exploration. When you're close to achieving your goal but need a bit more clarity or assurance, use the tools of engagement.

Let me show you how this works. My client Angelika had cleaned houses while studying for her real estate license. After passing the exam, she was hired by a national firm that teamed her up with a seasoned broker.

"Now that I'm on board," Angelika said, "I realize that I have a lot to learn about generating customers and selling. Mostly, I've been assisting my mentor as she stages open houses and guides potential buyers through the homes. Since passing my exam, the toughest thing has been comparing myself to others brokers. The good ones make it look so easy, and I forget that it took them years to build a referral base. My wake-up call was a sudden weight gain. As I pushed to get my own listings, my waistline started to expand, so I knew I was doing something wrong."

Like many people heading down a new path, Angelika was caught up in the notion that success means knowing everything all at once. Often, such individuals push themselves so hard that they fail to take the time to reflect on their unique style—and the ways they give added value to their customers. Angelika became hyperactive, then anxious, and then dug into a nice big piece of chocolate cake!

I said to Angelika, "Let's take the accent off the food and put it back on you. What is special about you and what you have to offer the customer?"

"People can trust me," she said. "After cleaning so many houses, I developed an innate sense that someone's home, no matter what the size, really is his or her castle. Now, as I try to find the right home for a particular client, I ask lots of questions, observe what interests the client, and listen—I don't push or impose. I treat each client like a king or queen!"

"So, your motto might be: Ask, observe, and listen."

From then on, Angelika used this motto daily, and she began to concentrate on cutting back her activities so she could focus on what she did best. Her anxiety lessened, and as she made new contacts, she soon discovered that she could fit comfortably into her clothes again!

KNOWING WHEN IT'S TIME TO ACT

A few years ago, Gabriella encouraged Amy and me to try the rowboat that came along with the condominium we were renting. So, one day, the three of us took the boat out and rowed through lily pads, passed ducks, saw a frog leap and splash, and skimmed through an inlet where we spotted minnows. When it was time for lunch, we headed back. As we bumped against the shore, I grabbed the towline, removed the oars, and jumped out of the boat. Gabriella followed, but Amy wavered, one foot on shore and the other in the boat.

"What do I do?" Amy yelled.

"Jump!" we replied.

She hesitated—and landed in the water. After she had dried off and recovered from her embarrassment, I asked, "Why didn't you jump when you had the chance?"

"I was afraid," she said.

Similarly, some of my clients get too comfortable exploring the pond—they've learned to enjoy the scenery and have become a bit complacent—so I tell them this story about Amy and suggest that the time has come for them to take a leap.

Most people genuinely enjoy experimenting with ideas, networking with others, and sorting through their options. They gain perspective on their life and articulate their fresh focus. However, some wait too long to engage, to start to act on their new goals. Toward the end of the exploration stage, these individuals—pinched for money and stretched for time—can become anxious and frustrated but remain reluctant to push off.

Let's eavesdrop on a conversation I had with my client Nina, who was hesitant to take the plunge.

"You've clarified that your focus is starting a decor business, and you've taken courses, interviewed people in the trade, and spoken with several of your friends," I said. "But you won't take the last step. Can you tell me why?"

"I'm afraid that if I finally open the door to my business, I'll fail," she said. "What if I lose all the money I've set aside? Then where will I be?"

"We need to figure out a way for you to feel confident about your risk. One of my clients, an architect, started running her new firm from her home and thus avoided signing an expensive lease. Instead, she spent the money on developing her customer base—by taking potential clients to lunch, for example. I know that your dream location is the downtown Design Center, but its premium rents will have you frantically running right off the bat. What can you do to make your launch more manageable?"

"Cliff, you're right. I need time to generate customers and to establish myself. I can operate from my home and take samples to residences and businesses. Besides, I'll be visiting the Design Center plenty with my new customers. Do you think I could meet with your other client to better understand how she set up her home business?"

"Yes, but you have the idea now." I told her the story about Amy and the rowboat. "You don't want to have one foot on land—focusing on customers—and the other in the boat—worrying about rent. You want to move ahead and plant both feet firmly on the shore."

DESCRIBING YOUR MISSION

When my clients feel clear about their strengths and are ready to take them out into the marketplace, I ask them to create a "Capability and Partnership Statement." The purpose of this is to build their confidence and position them as capable players looking for worthy partners. At this stage, the goals are to

- Explore desires and goals with managers, business owners, and customers, and commit to working *with* them on effective solutions

- Learn new skills and contribute to colleagues and customers

- Initiate and continue one's professional and personal growth

- Create relationships built on both mutual respect and the free exchange of information and ideas

- Own one's values and feel aligned with the company's vision or the customer's goals

You've come too far to chain yourself to a hierarchy or stay in a situation that keeps you dependent. This is the time for being proactive by taking an inventory of your assets and putting yourself forward in the best possible light.

Your Capability and Partnership Statement is a flexible, living document you can rewrite again and again as you grow and connect with the marketplace. The following figure contains an example—written by my client Jackson, an Englishman who has worked in the United States as a consultant in the field of information technology.

Jackson sent his statement to several colleagues and asked for their feedback. One commented, "The 'I' didn't come through enough. I didn't feel your personal drive and optimism." Another

CAPABILITY AND PARTNERSHIP STATEMENT

Objective. To transform a business with the mission of improving people's lives through the innovative and creative use of information technologies, with an emphasis on customer satisfaction, competitive strategies, and bottom-line results.

Partnership talents. I want to employ the following strengths:

- The capacity to see far ahead and then create paths that may lead to opportunities
- A can-do attitude toward overcoming hurdles and planning for business growth
- Current IT expertise and vast experience with practical applications
- A respect for others and the ability to lead and manage them
- A creative and collaborative approach to problem solving

Relevant results. I can offer the building blocks from my past, in which I

- Pioneered and successfully led an entrepreneurial venture that became a leader in the field of computer networking
- Sold the enterprise to a Fortune 100 company
- Led a small business unit within a large technology group
- Opened and developed the U.S. market for a European IT company

Partnership sought. I seek to join a company that is at its core

- *Innovative.* Creativity is put to work.

- *Entrepreneurial.* Risk and growth are fostered.

- *Open.* Questions, ideas, and debate are encouraged.

- *Values driven.* Everything possible to meet client needs is done.

- *Systems oriented.* Respect is maintained for the connection among all stakeholders: clients, investors, and staff members as well as the working environment.

said, "Show that personal philosophy that so many of us respect." Jackson then revised the document to include his personal statement, as shown in the following figure.

"As you know, I've had issues around self-confidence," he said, "and the personal statement put me on the line. The speech from the movie *Apollo 13* kept coming back to me: Failure is not an option. My family is depending on me, and I can't fail them. I need to have faith in myself and in what I'm doing, and this faith must come through to people in the marketplace. My Capability and Partnership Statement lets me share my intent with others."

In the subsequent weeks, Jackson tailored his Capability and Partnership Statement for different audiences. He sent it to his colleagues and associates with a brief note asking whether they knew of any opportunities that he might consider and asking them to keep their eyes open for future prospects. These people already trusted his integrity, work history, and education. When Jackson sent the Capability and Partnership Statement to smaller companies—where the

CAPABILITY AND PARTNERSHIP STATEMENT

Objective. To transform a business with the mission of improving people's lives through the innovative and creative use of information technologies, with an emphasis on customer satisfaction, competitive strategies, and bottom-line results.

Partnership talents. I want to employ the following strengths:
- The capacity to see far ahead and then create paths that may lead to opportunities
- A can-do attitude toward overcoming hurdles and planning for business growth
- Current IT expertise and vast experience with practical applications
- A respect for others and the ability to lead and manage them
- A creative and collaborative approach to problem solving

Relevant results. I can offer the building blocks from my past, in which I
- Pioneered and successfully led an entrepreneurial venture that became a leader in the field of computer networking
- Sold the enterprise to a Fortune 100 company
- Led a small business unit within a large technology group
- Opened and developed the U.S. market for a European IT company

Partnership sought. I seek to join a company that is at its core

- *Innovative.* Creativity is put to work.

- *Entrepreneurial.* Risk and growth are fostered.

- *Open.* Questions, ideas, and debate are encouraged.

- *Values driven.* Everything possible to meet client needs is done.

- *Systems oriented.* Respect is maintained for the connection among all stakeholders: clients, investors, and staff members as well as the working environment.

Personal statement. My life and leadership philosophy can be summed up as follows:

- My goal is to improve the lives of my colleagues, customers, coworkers, and stockholders, showing respect to all. I consider their needs, welcome their feedback, and generally deliver more than each constituency expects.

president seemed accessible—he added a cover letter that described how he would address their goals. For large corporations, Jackson included a traditional resume that documented his career history, specific responsibilities, and detailed accomplishments.

A few months later, Jackson moved back to England with his family. He bought into an existing construction company that was hungry for his skills in organizing information and using computer technology. A colleague who had received the Capability and Partnership Statement had made the introduction, noting that Jackson's personal philosophy was in alignment with that of the owners.

I urge you to write your own Capability and Partnership Statement to clarify your values and philosophy. Just take a moment and fill in the blanks.

CAPABILITY AND PARTNERSHIP STATEMENT

Objective.

Partnership talents.

Relevant results.

Partnership sought.

Personal statement.

Your Capability and Partnership Statement will steer you toward others who value your vision and clarity. This statement of intent is the culmination of your process of reflection and exploration. It reflects your values and describes the relationship you want to build with the outside world.

After you complete this document, you'll know how to approach others, and you'll also begin to see outer-economy returns. Essayist Roger Rosenblatt observed, "The best in art and life comes from a center, something urgent and powerful—an ideal or emotion that insists on its being. From that insistence a shape emerges and creates its structure out of passion." Don't try this in reverse, Rosenblatt cautions. "If you begin with a structure, you have to make up the passion. And that's very hard to do."

DEFINING YOUR ASSETS

Ganesh, a vice president for an off-price retailer, decided it was time to sail around the world. Already in his early 40s, he intended to pursue his childhood dream—and his family was all for it. To prepare for the voyage, he needed a flexible work schedule and a good salary for some months preceding the launch. He tried to renegotiate his hours with his employer, but the negotiation failed. Ganesh then sent an abbreviated version of his Capability and Partnership Statement, which is shown in the following figure, to the people in his network. After e-mailing this proposal to approximately thirty of his colleagues and associates, Ganesh landed a temporary assignment that would support him for the next eight months. After that, he was on his way around the world.

GANESH

Ganesh Ganguli, currently a vice president at off-price retailer Zarget, has unparalleled experience and expertise in the distribution and warehousing of goods. Because of future travel and family plans, he seeks a contract (up to a year) with another retailer to develop and/or manage its distribution operation.

Ganesh has grown his current plant from infancy to a state-of-the-art facility that operates in a fast-paced, globally competitive marketplace. He is an expert in planning and organizing high-functioning systems and in leading people to optimally manage those systems. Ganesh's hallmark is "getting the right goods to the stores on time."

If you know of any organization that might be interested in Ganesh's skills or of someone Ganesh might contact to further assist him in his search, please contact ganesh@xxx.com. Thank you.

MOVING AN 800-POUND ROCK

A few years ago, a freeze killed most of the shrubs in our front garden, prompting a complete redesign. I envisioned a Japanese motif—simple, with ground cover, stepping-stones, a few select bushes, and a large, relatively flat rock to act as the centerpiece. My search for the right rock started a minor buzz. Neighbors wondered how I would move a rock up and over the berm without destroying everything in the rock's path. I didn't worry. I figured that I had prepared the space and the rest would inevitably follow.

While visiting my favorite nursery, I spotted an irregular rock of gray granite—a low rectangle that was one foot high, three feet wide, and four feet long. A notch had been cut out from one corner—home for a dwarf bush. Delivery was promised in one week, and the following Saturday at 2:00 in the afternoon, I heard Gabriella yell, "Dad, the rock is here!"

The driver looked at me as if to say, "Now what?"

I asked, "Do you have a plan?"

"We used a crane to move this thing onto my truck," he said, "but all we have now is a crowbar, a four-wheel dolly, and a wagon."

I looked at the driver's partner. He offered no help. We all shrugged and then improvised a solution. The driver pushed a button on the dashboard, which tipped the bed of the truck so that the rock could slide onto the wagon and the dolly together. The idea was to distribute the weight of the rock as evenly as possible between the two. Very slowly, the driver inched the truck away as his partner and I guided the mass. When the bulk of the rock had slid off the truck, we noticed that the wagon's wheels had sunk halfway into the sod— and the three of us could not make them budge. By this time, a crowd had gathered, and people started coming forward to take up positions around the rock. With a "one, two, three," everyone pushed together. At that moment, I shoved the crowbar under one of the wheels and yanked it out of the sod. We freed each wheel in turn and then proceeded to advance, rolling the wagon and then the dolly—leaving a maze of zigzag ruts in the front lawn—until the gray rock had found its new home.

Moving that rock was a lot like developing an ideal job description. To begin, you must have a vision. And, even though you may have to zigzag quite a bit, you have to keep moving—trusting that others will come along to help you find just the right position for your rock.

VISUALIZING YOUR IDEAL SPACE

It's often helpful to envision the place you want to work in—and to be as specific as possible. As you circulate your Capability and Partnership Statement, develop the definition of your ideal environment. The following questions will help you visualize your perfect space, thus increasing the likelihood that your rock will drop into the right place for you:

- **Where is your ideal job located?** Site your garden. How many miles do you commute? How do you get there?

- **What does your ideal work environment look like?** Does it have bushes and ground cover? Is it well lit? Crowded? Solitary and serene? Vibrant and upbeat?

- **How does your work tap into your essence?** Are you using the skills you most prize? Are your hands in the earth, committed to practical tasks? Or, does your imagination run free because you're a blue-sky person who needs to be up in the clouds?

- **How do others treat you?** How do you interact with them?

- **How—and how much—do you travel?** Do you travel by train, airplane, pickup truck, or wagon, and where do you go?

- **What are you contributing?** Are you creating community and mentoring others? Will the world become a better place as a result of your contribution?

- **How do you feel at the end of the day?** Do you still like your team? Do you like the person you're becoming?

MAKING SMALL CHANGES, SEEING BIG REWARDS

Trim tabs are stabilizers attached to either side of the stern of a boat. When adjusted even slightly, they help the boat cruise much more efficiently by bringing it to plane and thus reducing the amount of drag in the water. When my clients head out into unfamiliar waters, I encourage them to look for trim tab adjustments—small changes they can make that can bring big rewards. Following are some examples.

––––––––

Challenge: *How do I distinguish myself from other candidates?*

Trim tab adjustment: Include a photograph that illuminates your personality. Many of my clients send a photograph with their Capability and Partnership Statement. Often, the picture they choose is a professional head shot—a photo devoid of a smile or any gesture reflecting their uniqueness.

Hire a photographer to take a candid shot—one that captures your personality. Would you want to do business with someone who looks warm and approachable or with a stone-faced character? My client Mack has a ready smile and enjoys wearing a necktie without a jacket. The tie knot is always skewed to the right. So, that is how he had his picture taken—with his face beaming and his tie characteristically off center.

———————

Challenge: *How do I show that I'm the most attractive partner?*

Trim tab adjustment: Be clear about how your strengths can benefit the organization. Companies large and small are interested in how you can solve their problems and work with their customers in a global marketplace that is increasingly competitive. They seek partners who are clear about how their strengths can benefit them.

Don't operate out of a job-description mentality that emphasizes title, position, and narrowly defined responsibilities. Focus on what you can do for the company's customers. Explain how you've worked to give added value to your customers. Show how your experience and skills are aligned with the company's needs. When Zulu, a financial controller, interviewed for a new position, he brought a colorful timeline he'd created to demonstrate the methods and processes he would use to both reduce the company's debt and allow for its expansion.

———————

Challenge: *How do I negotiate fairly for the highest possible salary?*

Trim tab adjustment: Wait for the gulp. Let's say that the salary range for a particular job is $75,000 to $85,000. All the other aspects of the job fit for you. Now, it's time to land a salary at the upper end of the range—remembering that once you accept any job, increases are usually painfully small and slow in coming.

After you say, "I'm excited about this job and would appreciate a salary at the top end of this range," remain calm and say nothing. As tough as this is, wait for the gulp. When the interviewer sweats for a bit and then breaks the silence, you will get paid what you deserve.

———————

_____

Challenge: *How do I get an indecisive employer off the fence?*

Trim tab adjustment: Ask point blank. For example, let's say you have other job possibilities but are most excited about this one—and they've been hedging for a month. You feel strongly about your value to this employer.

Take control. Call the hiring manager and say, "It's been a month since our last meeting, all of the signals seemed positive, and in most ways we've agreed that I can add significant value to your organization and your customers. I have one question: Are you going to hire me?" Jaya, a graphic designer for the Internet, tried this tack. The manager laughed and said, "Come into my office tomorrow so you can sign our letter of agreement."

_____

Challenge: *How do I increase my passion and productivity?*

Trim tab adjustment: When necessary, buy yourself some time. A common complaint is that much of the work day is eaten up by trivial tasks. As one director of marketing said, "I've taken on one detail after another and I'm drowning in minutiae. I can't get to what I love—nurturing customer relationships and developing strategic plans."

When colleagues, customers, partners, and your boss are piling on demands, you can buy yourself some time by saying, "Let me think about that, and I'll get back to you." Don't immediately say yes to everything. Take a moment to consider whether your talents are best suited to the particular project. Chances are that at least some of these tasks can be resolved by other means.

Genuine engagement is possible only if your role in the outer economy is truly right for you. The suggestion to buy yourself time is not a prescription for setting rigid boundaries within which you never accept a

THE COURAGE TO ENGAGE

less-than-perfect task. Instead, it's an approach that can help you stay on the path of greater flexibility and productivity. When you take control of your position by adjusting the trim tabs, more often than not you add value to others by doing what you do best.

LOOKING BENEATH THE SPLATTER

At a secondhand store in Brooklyn, I spotted a four-legged yellow stool splattered with brown, red, white, and green paint. An artist had probably used it as a makeshift easel, and hundreds of customers had passed it up, put off by the hodgepodge of colors. My family thought I was nuts, but I asked the vendor, "How much?"

"Twelve dollars," he said.

"Seven," I countered.

We settled on nine. I noticed that bystanders were now eyeing the stool. It had instantly gained value because it was no longer for sale. Continuing to stroll, I envisioned the stool's many uses: as an extra seat, part-time plant stand or ladder, and aesthetic object for the discerning eye.

My paint-splattered stool helped Shane, a specialist in business acquisitions, make a liberating decision for his company.

"Another division has an employee who's troubled," Shane said, "and my boss decided to place him under my management. Everybody sees me as the compassionate, mentoring type. However, I'm in the midst of developing a high-performance team, so dumping this guy on me will end up not only draining my time but also derailing my efforts."

"What would you like to say to your boss about this?" I asked.

"I'm upset that he made this decision along with the senior vice president without consulting me. I've worked hard to build my team, and I don't want to take on the burden of somebody who will weigh us down."

"You have good reasons to feel upset. Bear with me for a moment, and let me tell you about the value of noticing things that other people overlook." I told Shane the story of the paint-splattered stool.

"Gems often come camouflaged," I said. "Is there a way for you to engage the situation on your own terms, perhaps to conceive a solution that others have passed by?"

Shane began to picture the employee as misguided rather than flawed. He felt that the employee's boss needed to communicate with him in a better way, rather than passing the buck to another manager.

Shane said, "I'm going to propose that I step forward as an internal coach to both the employee and his boss. Under my plan, the employee will remain under his boss's wing, and I'll help them both deepen their sense of responsibility and enhance their collaboration. I'll make your point, Cliff, that one of my abilities is seeing beneath the surface splatter and coming up with new alternatives."

TRUSTING THAT HELP WILL COME

I hopped into a cab at my hotel and headed for the U.S. Department of the Interior, where I was to give a talk about developing the inner economy. The driver, who was from Uganda, asked what I was doing in D.C. I told him I was giving a talk to government officials about how to become happier and more productive. Then, I asked him, "What do you think of working in the United States?"

Without hesitation, he replied, "Working in America is good. I've been here for less than ten years, and already I own a home. My parents and one of my brothers live with me."

"That's quite an accomplishment. You must have worked hard for your home."

"It's not enough to work hard," he said. "You've got to know the system. I drive this cab ten—sometimes fifteen—hours a day. Driving a cab does not pay for my house."

"What do you mean by 'know the system?'"

"My father taught his sons that if they believed in themselves, they could attain their dreams. I believed that I could make a better life for my family and myself, and my dream came true. I didn't spend all my money; I learned how to invest it. I heard the big shots in the back of my cab talking about the stock market, so I asked one of them, 'If I had some money to invest, would you show me how?' I saved my money and took the right shot. I got lucky."

"Anything else?" I asked.

"My family needed a car, and my Papa liked the Lexus. I would hear people in the back of my cab talk about their cars. One guy said that a Lexus is expensive and it's just a Toyota in disguise. So, I convinced Papa to buy an Avalon. He likes it, and my family saved money."

"To invest?"

"Right."

The title of my talk that morning was "We Are All Self-Employed: How to Take Control of Your Career." I began, "It's not enough to work hard; you've got to know the system. On my way from my hotel room to this building, I was driven by a cabby from Uganda who came here ten years ago and now has money in the bank and owns his own home. His advice was as good as any that I have come to give today: You have to have a dream. Next, you must believe in your dream and in yourself. Then, save your money and spend it wisely. Finally, trust that others can help you make your dream come true."

No one knows everything; everyone needs to trust someone.

GRASPING THAT TIME IS NOT THE ENEMY

At Inspiration Point in Yellowstone National Park, I stood at least a thousand feet above the crusted rock and rushing river. I felt I could see forever, and, in a moment of clarity, I saw the bare bones of my life and understood what matters the most. Back home in Boston, I tried to hold on to this perspective—despite my penchant for over-scheduling and taking on too many projects.

This story came in handy when my client Bethany felt overwhelmed, yet continued to place even more demands on herself. She was no longer interested in teaching her school arts program but wanted to do something that would both foster her creativity and give her time to raise her family. She was eager to begin training for a different kind of future.

I asked Bethany, "Have you ever been to Inspiration Point at Yellowstone?"

"Yes," she said, "It's unforgettable, isn't it? We were there just a few weeks ago."

"What a spot for gaining perspective on life. We can too easily convince ourselves that we have to respond to everyone and everything. All those demands can get a little tiring."

"I know what you mean," said Bethany. "Up there, I felt free—almost as though I could fly."

"Free from what?" I asked.

"I feel overwhelmed by my children's needs and frustrated by my desire to press on toward a new job. When I'm at home, the two pressures seem to collide, with each one vying for my full attention. When I was at Inspiration Point, I had the thought that if I attended to my own dreams, I'd be happier and freer to give to my children."

"What blocks you from bringing Inspiration Point back home?"

Bethany said, "I lose perspective as I race to attend to details. Then, I get frustrated and discouraged and feel really drained."

"One of the thoughts I had at Inspiration Point was that this wonderland had been carved by time. Wind, rain, and fire carved out the canyon, etched the rock, and fertilized the vegetation. In modern life, we don't allow ourselves this kind of long-range perspective. Instead, we cut the journey short with the expectation that results are everything—and that these results must come immediately. We forget that life is a journey, and that each achievement is just one step along the way."

"I like this philosophy, but how do I apply it to my situation?"

"In your life, you've explored many things—from cooking, to flower arranging, to meditation, to dance. Now, ask yourself this: How can you create a bridge between your work and personal lives? Bring your job choice closer to home. Make it not only a means of self-expression but also the result of a process that includes your family."

During the next year, Bethany taught art part-time and took several types of dance classes, including tango, salsa, and classic waltz. Her husband became her waltz partner, and her children signed up for hip-hop and disco lessons. While her family was having fun, Bethany was deciding whether to become a dance instructor.

Bethany said, "Sometimes after dinner, I play our favorite Motown CD. My kids boogie to "How Sweet It Is to Be Loved by

You," and my husband gets nostalgic with "Ain't No Mountain High Enough." I fly when I tango, and I'm thinking that I would love to teach it. But, I would never have taken a step in this direction if we hadn't first talked about perspective."

USING PINBALL WIZARDRY

As I approached age 50, my doctor advised me to have a colonoscopy. On the day of the procedure, I was a little anxious. Before we got started, I asked the doctor, "How many of these do you perform in a day?"

"Between four and six."

"How do you train for this sort of thing? I've heard that the colon is a very tender area."

"Since undergraduate school," the doctor said, "I've played video games. I find they help develop my dexterity."

My brother Geoff recently called to inform me that he, too, was preparing for a colonoscopy. I assured him that it's a routine procedure, and I advised him to ask whether his doctor was a pinball wizard!

Over the years, I've taught my clients that there are many ways to hone one's skills and stay engaged. Here are just a few.

- Teach an adult education class to share your expertise.

- Mentor or tutor someone who could use your help.

- Form or join a professional group to air your concerns and hear the solutions that others propose.

- Write about your ideas and discoveries, and submit an article to a newsletter, newspaper, or magazine.

- Volunteer to speak about your discoveries and perspectives at an association meeting or convention.

- Rollerblade, cycle, or walk to work as a means not only of staying in shape but also of clearing your mind before you have to play the game of office politics for the day.

- Become idea prone: combine old skills and talents in new ways.

- Remind yourself why you've engaged in an ongoing journey of rethinking your work.

UNCOVERING THE KEY TO STAYING POWER

Staying power is not the ability to sweat things out just because that's what good soldiers do but the commitment to keep on exploring your work and your true character. This commitment doesn't always mean changing jobs. Sometimes, it means staying right where you are and learning how to challenge yourself and your colleagues so you don't get stuck in old routines.

My dentist, Jim, has grown his business for seventeen years by keeping up-to-date on his patients' interests. He's emotionally available and takes the time to really listen. To stay intellectually active, he teaches the latest techniques in dentistry at the local medical and dental school. He also shares new approaches with his staff and his partners, and his reputation as a researcher draws in even more patients. Some of Jim's other strategies include

- **Giving public lectures.** Jim informs the community about the latest dentistry techniques and how he applies them in his practice. In a more general vein, he asks for people's opinions about our overall health care system.

- **Mentoring and teaching.** Jim encourages others in his field to upgrade their knowledge and skills.

- **Maintaining a library.** Jim shares his collection of books on government, management, world affairs, and leadership principles with his staff and his patients. When I went in for a cleaning, Jim asked, "Is Wal-Mart a blessing? What do you think, Cliff?" He handed me *The Wal-Mart Effect* by Charles Fishman to take home. The next time I visit Jim, I'm sure he'll ask for my opinion.

HONING YOUR VISION OF THE FUTURE

Writing this book involved thousands of tasks and carried me through the three-step process of reflecting, exploring, and engaging. I felt tremendously nourished by the daily practice of sitting down to compose my thoughts and describe the nature of my work. However, a whole different set of skills was required to bring the book out into the world. My process of engagement provides a useful model for discussion.

After completing the writing part of *Rethinking Work*, I needed to

- **Secure endorsements.** I needed to call people I knew—and didn't know—to ask if they'd review my book, in the hope that their opinions and signatures would bolster sales.

- **Find matches among companies, universities, and associations.** Finding such matches required calling these organizations, introducing *Rethinking Work* to them, and discovering whether my message aligned with their values. When a match occurred, I'd propose giving a presentation or keynote address at an off-site meeting or divisional retreat.

- **Contact the media.** Carrying out this activity meant getting in touch with newspapers, radio stations, television stations, and Internet portals regarding interviews and speaking opportunities.

- **Develop special events.** I had to cultivate book signings, small dinners, and group presentations where I could share my ideas, generate visibility, and stimulate sales.

- **Remain open to unexpected requests.** Such requests could range from individual consultations to customized trainings to adaptations of my book into other products, such as workbooks, Internet-accessible questionnaires, and CD-ROMs.

- **Update my Web site.** I thought it important that my Web site be better aligned with the content of *Rethinking Work*.

- **Overall, shift into outer-economy activity.** At the same time, I could never lose sight of the fact that I am a steward of my message and must live what I preach. My goal would continue to be becoming wiser—and supporting others in looking at work from the inside out.

Engagement raises the bar and increases personal risk. It also requires us to reflect on our original intentions to make sure we haven't gotten sidetracked along the way.

REVISITING THE BASICS

During this final stage of engaging the world, it's a good idea to go back to the basics and reexplore your definition of success. As you're considering new opportunities and marketplace demands, you don't want to lose sight of the ideals that motivated you to make a change in the first place, nor do you want to get knocked off balance.

I've already told you about my client Sandra, who left her job as a grant writer to work with ceramic tile. She worked her way up from subcontractor to contractor, registered her business officially, hired two assistants to lighten her load, and received five-star ratings on a popular Web site. She came back to see me a year later, with her assistant Debi, to discuss ways to expand her business. Here are her key questions:

- What am I really selling?

- What kind of business do I want to build?

- How do I define success?

Our discussions around these questions are described in the following sections.

Clarifying What You're Really Selling

"In my trade, people can be sloppy," Sandra said. "They lay new tile onto warped floorboards or recommend the wrong materials. We do our research and pay attention to detail; we've thus gained a reputation for fixing the jobs others have already botched."

"Clearly, tiling involves much more than simply placing and cementing a bunch of stones," I replied. "First, you do your research by scoping out the project. Then, you consider a plan, which includes labor and materials, to produce a result of high quality. But, what are you selling that's unique?"

To answer that question, I suggested that Sandra and Debi tell each other detailed stories about how they perform on the job. The intent of these stories is not to judge individual or team performance but to observe and become better acquainted with the methods each person prefers to use. During this exercise, the women would write down the words and phrases that best described their work. These expressions might include

- Problem solving

- Plotting and patching

- Organizing tools and buying supplies

- Being punctual

- Generating creative ideas and solutions

- Checking in with customers when questions arise

- Explaining activities

- Coming up with affordable solutions

My second suggestion was that Sandra interview five or six of her customers and ask them what they appreciated most about her service. Here, too, key words and phrases would be plucked from each story—illuminating the value of the work Sandra and her crew delivered.

With two sets of feedback, Sandra would be able to describe the essence of her business. Marketers refer to this as *branding;* they use branding catch phrases to position and sell a service.

Clarifying the Kind of Business You Want to Build

Sandra said, "Although we are frequently called to redo unsatisfactory work, my heart isn't in repairing what others have messed up. We are artists, and we have our own creative vision. I'm a quilter, Debi is a singer, and my other assistant, Ethan, is a painter. My ideal would be to take on a variety of home improvement jobs, such as helping a customer design a unique patio or unusual hearth."

"Have you completed any original designs to date?" I asked.

"We've done three or four small jobs. Although they take the most thought, they have brought me the most joy. They tie together my analytical, creative, and practical sides."

I recommended that Sandra ask her customers if she might photograph their installations and that she then build a Web site featuring these "practical yet creative" artisan projects.

Sandra commented, "What if there's not enough creative work out there or if it just trickles in? How will I pay my bills?"

"Pay your bills *and* live your dream," I said. "It's not an either-or situation. Continue to take on repair jobs and standard jobs while letting potential customers know about your specialty. You'll want to direct all your potential customers to your new Web site. You might also have special postcards printed that show your creative projects. Use them as business cards that you send through the mail to announce your new services and to share fresh ideas. You might offer potential clients a free consultation and, on the back end, thank your existing customers for continuing to maintain their trust in you."

"I understand," Sandra said. "My dream will become a reality if we find ways to balance the financial bottom line with our creative desires."

Clarifying Your Definition of Success

"I have all kinds of questions that concern understanding my definition of success," Sandra said. "How big do I want my business to get? Do I want to eventually sell it? How much of the time do I want to be physically involved, working with the stone, versus designing and managing my crew? What will I need to let go of in the other parts of my life in order to make more money? Am I willing to sacrifice time with my family to build a bigger business?"

"You are asking good and necessary questions," I noted. "Every one of them is critical to a fuller engagement. You say you need to tie your analytical, creative, and practical sides together. It seems that success for you has much to do with integrating these parts of yourself. Henry David Thoreau said, "Dwell as near as possible to the channel in which your life flows." Instead of racing toward the answers to all your questions, why not experience more of the analytical, creative, and practical flow that makes you feel so alive?"

Sandra has since discovered that the process of engagement is both exhilarating and never ending. She has begun to notice when the three parts of her personality are all in play and what projects are most likely to engage them all. As the outer world screams, "Plow ahead. Go for the money," she is taking the time to savor her experience. As a result, she continues to feel excited about her journey and her work. "If I've learned anything," she says, "it's to listen to my instincts and then do my homework. When I defer to others' expectations, I end up disappointed. Having listened to myself, I'm building something for myself."

—— Check-In ——

THE COURAGE TO ENGAGE

Here are some writing exercises that will help you clarify your plan of action. If you get stuck at any point during the engagement phase, don't hesitate to review these questions and revise your answers. Remember that your journey is a work in progress and that you can reuse these tools at many different points throughout your life.

Here are the check-in questions for you to answer:

- What practical steps must you take to launch your dream?

- How can you assimilate the quality of "adding value to others' lives" and make it a part of your work?

- How does your Capability and Partnership Statement help you reach your target audience and make your mission known to others? And, how does it increase your productivity on the job?

- What are you selling or proposing to others that will improve their lives?

- How, specifically, are you engaging the world—and how is the marketplace responding?

- What can you do to increase your chances of success? How can making trim tab adjustments help?

AFTERWORD

DON'T WAIT FOR THE FUTURE

LIVE FULLY NOW

We tend to postpone being alive to the future,
the distant future, we don't know when.
THICH NHAT HANH

On a raw New England fall day, teeming rain mixed with the kind of wind that pricks and stings your cheeks. It was an utter mess outside; but, rather than merely shiver and complain, I decided to go about my business and heed Anne Frank's advice, "Nobody needs to wait a single moment before starting to improve the world."

At the bank, I held the door open for a gentleman who was scurrying up the steps behind me. He looked at my wet face with a mixture of gratitude and disbelief. When I later went shopping, I noticed that the cashier seemed overwhelmed by the long line of customers, so I began to bag my groceries. As she helped me load them into my cart, she touched my shoulder and said, "Thanks."

That evening, Amy asked, "How was your day?"

I answered, "Great!"

I've learned to inch closer toward my vision of a wiser, more joyful world that is freer, safer, and filled with more possibilities for all. This vision acts as the guiding principle that I offer my clients—and that I want to offer you—as you search for more meaningful and fulfilling work.

At every point along your journey—whether you're launching a new career or just starting to rethink your relationship to work—you need to allow each moment to expand to its full potential. Doing so means going forth with good intentions and an open heart.

As a boy, I landscaped yards and painted houses. These jobs allowed me to work in the glorious outdoors and to set my own schedule. I concentrated all my efforts on whoever was my current customer—knowing that if I did my best, the job would lead me to another.

Now, more than thirty years later, my business deliverables are quite different, but my vision remains intact. I typically take on four to seven new clients a month, and my goal is to be present emotionally, spiritually, and intellectually for all of them. When a client feels clearer, calmer, and more confident as a result of our work, he or she is likely to send a friend, colleague, or boss in for consultation, too.

The problem is that many people focus so greatly on some distant goal that they lose the joy of being in the current moment.

PRESSING ONE DIGIT AT A TIME

Traveling through life one step at a time can be challenging. When my client Heidi tried to straighten out a credit card bill, she got frustrated by the automated phone system. "When I finally figured out how to navigate it," she noted, "the automated voice said, 'Please enter your account number, one digit at a time.' Is there any other way to do it?"

I tell my clients, "Just handle one call, one cover letter, and one interview at a time. The job search can be daunting, so investigate your options slowly and methodically. One opportunity will always lead you to another."

After many months of reflection, Gustavo, a research specialist, took the leap and gave notice to his employer. "A small environmental research firm has enough work for me to do through the end of the year." he said. "With my savings, I can survive a bit longer than that while I look for other work."

"How do you feel about your decision?" I asked.

"Extremely happy. I feel quite excited, a little nervous, and suddenly more confident that other work will come and that, if anything, I'll be busier than ever before."

SHARING YOUR WEALTH

When Shaquana spoke about leaving her job, she seemed a little short of breath.

I asked, "How are you feeling now?"

"I'm afraid to tell my boss and colleagues that I have a new position. They will probably take my leaving personally."

"Will you breathe easier if you let them know that you're not fleeing from them or the company but moving toward an opportunity that feels earned and right at this stage of your life?"

"Yes, I will breathe easier if I speak up and say, 'All of you have been important in my life development. My choice to leave does not take one bit away from my experience here; rather, it's a compliment based on what I've learned from you.'"

As my client Kelvin prepared to leave a twenty-year law partnership, he decided to share his story, too. He told me that he wanted to do three things: thank his colleagues by telling them how much he appreciated their talents and dedication, reassure his clients that all their concerns would be tended to before his departure, and maintain strong connections with his friends and associates in the legal field as he embarked on his new career.

Kelvin said, "When I announce my departure, some of the associates may become frightened, thinking that something must be wrong with this place now that the boss is leaving. My plan is to share my journey with them."

"What will you say?" I asked.

"My work at this firm has honed my skills and confidence to the point that I'm ready for the next stage of my life. I'm 48 years old and have always wanted to work in the retail industry. My dad was a merchant, and now I plan to open a specialty food and wine shop with my son and daughter. I'd really like for all of you to visit."

"Sounds like you've already assembled a guest list for a wine and cheese party—which could also generate some initial customers!"

HONORING YOUR CONNECTIONS

Ellie, a certified financial planner, was so preoccupied with attracting new clients that she lost sight of those who were already depending on her.

I asked, "How much of your time do you spend worrying about building up your clientele?"

"Most of it," she replied.

"Then, how is it possible for you to serve your current clients?"

"Oh, once I assess someone's needs and plug them into a program, not much more is required other than periodically reviewing that person's portfolio."

"But the markets are in constant flux today. If I were one of your high-end clients, I'd want more of your time and expertise."

"I wouldn't have it to give to you."

"The trouble is that you've flipped your focus. You're so worried about the future and how to build the business that you give your existing clients short shrift. If you were to invest more time in them—show them that you value them—they would then start referring others to you. You'd spend less time plotting how to attract new business and feel happier about your daily work."

"Do you mean, no more marketing?"

"Not at all. I'm suggesting that you shift your attitude for the next few weeks. Try putting 70 percent of your effort into client service. If you don't see an upsurge in your referrals, you can try another tack."

I drew a spiral on the whiteboard in my office and placed a dot, which represented one of Ellie's present clients, in the center of it. I asked her to tell me how she might spend more time helping this particular individual. As she spoke, I drew five other dots along the spiral (see the following figure) and explained, "This spiral corresponds to a timeline for the development of your business. As you work with the client in the center, her trust will deepen and she'll thus become more satisfied. The other dots represent five of her referrals."

Ellie said, "Now, that's a different orientation!"

"Exactly. Remember that your dreams are rooted in the same garden as your clients' dreams. When you help them achieve their goals, seeds will spread and more plants will sprout."

Ellie's Time-and-Development Line

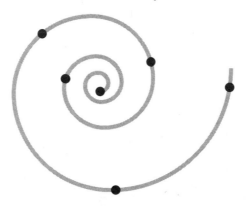

UPDATING YOUR BELIEFS

My best friend, Vin, brought wonder into people's lives. Once, when we went to a restaurant, Vin brought his own wineglasses in their original box. Carefully, he unpacked four of them as other patrons began to stare. The glasses were about three times the standard size. The waiter poured the wine. Vin then angled his glass, holding it up to the light to examine the color of the wine. He swirled the liquid to release its bouquet and burrowed his nose into the bowl. Others in the restaurant smiled and soon started swirling their glasses, too. Vin turned the mundane into the extraordinary for his friends, for onlookers, and, most of all, for himself.

We all have the opportunity to make magic every day. *Rethinking Work* was inspired by and written for people like you, who expect a lot from life and from themselves. As you begin to challenge yourself in new ways, you'll become a freer and happier person. Carl Rogers, the father of humanistic psychology, said "The good life is a process, not a state of being. It is a direction not a destination."

The most significant turning points occur when we question our hand-me-down beliefs. Although some of these beliefs may work for us, others may have become impediments to our everyday communications and obstacles to our mobility. George, a project manager, said, "I grew up believing that I should tell it like it is, so I give direct feedback at any cost. During my most recent performance review, I learned that some of my direct reports are afraid of me. When I probed deeper, I discovered that these people cringe whenever I give feedback; they say I lack compassion."

"How do you mean?" I asked.

"Well, no matter what one of my staff members is doing or who else is around, I unleash by telling that person what they are doing wrong, and then I correct him or her."

"How do you think that makes them feel?"

"Demeaned. When my boss gave me the review, he said, 'Afraid.'"

"It seems that 'Tell it like it is' has been your creed for some time."

"My father was brutally honest about everything. Although I am a chip off the old block, I need to update my belief that this is the only way to be. I know that I can give helpful feedback—in fact, it is my job to do so. Maybe my new creed can be, 'Tell it the way others might hear it better.'"

"Yes, it's all a question of nuance. What might I see you doing as you follow through on your updated belief?"

"Right off the bat," George said, "I'll ask my staff member, 'Is now a good time to talk?' Also, if I'm anxious about something, I'll try not to agitate others. I'll modulate my voice—or wait until I've cooled down to talk. You know, I'll perform the old counting to ten! Furthermore, I'll make sure to praise people more by letting them know what they're doing to contribute to the project. And there's one more thing. I'll ask more questions, such as 'What do you like best about the way you perform that task?' and, 'What might be another way to approach that problem?'"

"It sounds like you've taken your review to heart. Remember to give yourself some leeway while you practice. It will take others a while to trust your new methods and some time for you to adjust to and feel comfortable with your emerging management style. One last question: How will you know your approach is working?"

"People's eyes won't get so big when I walk toward them," George said. "They'll come to me more often with their questions and concerns. I'll hear more laughter and, hopefully, my year-end review will read 'caring and productive,' not just 'laser-focused and demanding.'"

George's old beliefs were limiting his effectiveness and his ability to motivate and inspire others. "If you don't change your beliefs, your life will be like this forever," wrote Somerset Maugham. "Is that good news?"

Success often stems from replacing old ideas with new ones that will work better. For many of my clients, that means replacing a competitive or adversarial way of relating to the world with one of trust and openness.

The following table contains examples of how we can transform our thinking and move out into the world with greater ease and grace. It shows how we can update our beliefs and develop new behaviors that will benefit us and everyone around us. Really, the table contains just a few examples of ways we can live in the present rather than operate out of our old, outworn, assumptions. Another benefit is that no out-of-pocket costs are associated with examining and changing our old beliefs!

THE GOOD NEWS GAZETTE

OLD BELIEF	UPDATED BELIEF	THE GOOD NEWS
• It's all or nothing.	• Thoughtful moderation could help my relationships.	• I will be able to clarify my position and remain open to others' feedback.
• Reflection is a waste of time.	• Taking stock of my inner economy is an active part of my business and personal growth.	• I will have the room to pause and ask myself, If I do x, will I become happier? Will the situation improve?
• Being happy at work means living without stress.	• Happiness requires risk taking, which in turn requires that I overcome my fears.	• I will be in a position to share my vision with the people I trust.
• Overplanning ensures success.	• Planning needs to be supplemented by staying flexible and open to contributions, even surprises, from others.	• I will be able to follow the unexpected twists that each project takes by welcoming new partners and approaches.
• My story doesn't count.	• To appreciate my worth is to honor my experience.	• I will be able to tell others about the things that inspire and excite me.

THE GOOD NEWS GAZETTE *cont'd*

OLD BELIEF	UPDATED BELIEF	THE GOOD NEWS
• Others control my schedule.	• Managing my time involves caring for my needs as well as those of others.	• I will have given myself permission to turn off my cell phone at dinner-time and then pay attention to my family.

BECOMING PATIENT WITH YOURSELF

Many years ago, I took a workshop on personal growth. The facilitator lined us up on a basketball court and asked each of us to choose a position, at the 15-, 12-, 8-, 5-, or 3-foot mark, and then to try and sink the ball. We each had three turns and could adjust our shooting distance at every turn. The scoring went like this: If you shot from 15 feet and sank the ball, you would receive 15 points; if you shot from 8 feet and sank the ball, you would receive 8 points; and so on. The participant who got the highest total score would be the winner.

I stood at 12 feet and took my best shot, but no luck. The next person shot from 5 feet and popped the ball right in. I took my second shot from 12 feet and missed again. Finally, I scored from 8 feet, but that was pure luck because I had no confidence left by then.

When everyone had finished, the facilitator requested that we take a seat on the bleachers, and then asked, "What did you learn?" Here are some of the responses:

- "You offered each of us a blank check, and we each paid ourselves contingent on our beliefs. I knew that if I shot from 3 feet and sank the ball, my confidence would build. Then, I could advance to 5 feet and then 8. My strategy was to go for incremental gains, and my final score was 16."

- "I went for the whole enchilada and stuck with that plan. It was all or nothing on every try, and I ended up with nothing. I've got to take a hard look at the way I'm wired and at what I define as winning."

- "After two unsuccessful shots, I moved from 12 feet to 5 feet and then scored. If I had moved from 12 feet after the first shot, I'd probably have scored 10 overall. Although we were competing among ourselves for the highest score, my greatest competition was with myself."

This experience taught me a good deal about my way of achieving my goals. Over the years, I've shifted to a kinder approach. I'm more introspective now and content to live with incremental changes. I've learned that I benefit by taking things one step at a time and allowing myself to strengthen my muscles—rather than jumping off the mark every single time. Ultimately, I find that I enjoy myself more at every step along the way.

EMBRACING THE NEXT STAGE OF YOUR LIFE

Peter Drucker warns, "By the time you catch up to change, the competition is ahead of you." The doomsayers think we should all prepare for unemployment. The recent spate of resizing and outsourcing only reinforces the belief that preparation is prudent. I want to take the focus off the market facilitators, cultural changes, and environmental shifts and put it back on you.

In the past decade, we have seen a proliferation of Internet job search engines, such as Monster.com, Jobster.com, Market10.com, SimplyHired.com, and Veritude.com. Despite the growth of these companies and the popularity of their services, using online job sites doesn't guarantee finding a right-fit job. True success relies, first, on taking charge of your inner economy development—clarity of focus and authentic expression of strengths and values; and then on combining these elements with outer economy needs—matching the benefits you bring to the company and/or its customers.

Of course, it is important that we become more aware of our shifting personal needs and desires. At the same time, however, population growth, increasing urbanization, immigration issues, alternative energy demands, global climate changes, and an increased worldwide communication capacity reinforce and lead us to a broader, more basic question: How do we create our future?

This is what I tell my clients: Understand that you'll have to rethink your relationship to work again and again. Use the tools of reflecting, exploring, and engaging to make sure you stay at the center of the process.

By reflecting, you'll learn to avoid blindly jumping into the next job and, instead, to first examine who you are and what you value. Benjamin Hoff, in *The Tao of Pooh*, said we shouldn't "be carried along by circumstances. . . . The Way of Self-Reliance starts with recognizing who we are, what we've got to work with, and what works best for us."

By exploring, you'll learn that money isn't the only variable in job decision making. You'll begin to look for work that matches your spirit and to find people and organizations that support you in your work and life quests.

By engaging, you'll learn about balance, collaboration, and perseverance. Your achievements—such as finding a new career, patenting your invention, advancing to the position of vice president, or selling your next script—won't define your happiness. Instead, they'll be the stepping-stones in your creative process.

My challenge to you is this: Don't wait for someone to hand you the perfect job. You can make your own magic. You can create your future. Why not get started now?

USING YOUR EDGE

To rethink your work, use your edge—your understanding of your inner economy. Doing so will keep you from teetering on the edge of the outer economy. Listen to your inner voice: Clarify what you need and want. Shine light on your fears and learn how to see past them. Become a pioneer in your inner and outer economies. By using this approach, you'll find that you have the wisdom and the skill to live your dreams.

If you've done the exercises in this book, you've received validation for your progress, as you deepened your understanding of transition, change, and growth, and you've moved beyond conventional limits and definitions.

To meet the challenges of a changing economy, keep applying the three basic principles: Seize your right to reflect, give yourself permission to explore, and develop your courage to engage. You can continue to create your future, based on your values, and to find joy in the years ahead.

BIBLIOGRAPHY

Listed below are the primary works I referred to in writing *Rethinking Work*. Of course, many others have influenced my thinking. To all of their authors, I am grateful.

Bardwick, Judith M. *The Plateauing Trap*. New York: AMACOM, 1986.

Coelho, Paulo. *The Alchemist*. San Francisco: HarperCollins, 1994.

Dunn, Paul, and Ron Baker. *The Firm of the Future*. Hoboken, NJ: Wiley, 2003.

Fishman, Charles. *The Wal-Mart Effect*. New York: Penguin Press, 2006.

Frankl, Viktor E. *Man's Search for Meaning*. New York: Washington Square Press, 1946.

Handy, Charles. *The Age of Unreason*. Boston: Harvard Business School Press, 1989.

———. *The Hungry Spirit*. New York: Broadway Books, 1998.

Hoff, Benjamin. *The Tao of Pooh*. New York: Penguin Books, 1982.

Jacobsen, Mary H. *Hand-Me-Down Dreams*. New York: Three Rivers Press, 1999.

Levoy, Gregg. *Callings*. New York: Harmony Books, 1997.

Nhat Hanh, Thich. *Being Peace*. Berkeley, CA: Parallax Press, 1987.

Peck, Scott M. *The Road Less Traveled*. New York: Simon and Schuster, 1978.

Shapiro, David A. *Choosing the Right Thing to Do*. San Francisco: Berrett-Koehler, 1999.

Vaillant, George E. *Aging Well*. New York: Little, Brown, 2002.

Zohar, Danah, and Ian Marshall. *Connecting with Our Spiritual Intelligence*. New York: Bloomsbury, 2000.

INDEX

ABOUT THE AUTHOR

Cliff Hakim is the founder of Rethinking Work®, a career consulting and strategy firm in Arlington, Massachusetts. He has pioneered the concept of the inner economy and lectured widely on his new approach—which involves teaching people to step outside the box, to know themselves, and to reinvent their relationships to work and creativity. The U.S. Department of the Interior cited Hakim's business best seller, *We Are All Self-Employed: How to Take Control of Your Career* (2nd ed., Berrett-Koehler, 2004), as its 2005 Career Book Choice. Hakim writes and publishes *rethinkingWork*®, a career column that focuses on putting the individual in charge of his or her job and career—no matter what changes are taking place in that person's organization or in the marketplace. A noted seminar leader, Hakim has given major presentations to Boeing Corporation, Bank Boston, Massachusetts Healthcare Association, and CFET (a human resources agency in Port-au-Prince, Haiti), as well as at Boston College, Tufts, Harvard, John F. Kennedy University, and Clarke University.

CONTACT INFORMATION

To inquire about individual career consulting, a corporate subscription to the *rethinkingWork*® column, or a seminar or presentation for your organization or association, contact Cliff Hakim at cliff@rethinkingwork.com or 617-661-1250. A checklist for customized career consulting appears on the following page for your individual use. This checklist is based on the variety of challenges that Rethinking Work clients have raised.

RETHINKING WORK®
Customizable Career Consulting

Cliff Hakim will show you how to take charge of your job and career as you, your company, and the marketplace change.

Here is your checklist for customized career consulting. Check the item if you want to

- ☐ Establish a fresh career focus and a plan to materialize your goals
- ☐ Develop a business proposal and a system to attract clients
- ☐ Determine how to leave a current business partner or employer on amicable terms
- ☐ Negotiate a severance package, salary increase, or shift in responsibilities
- ☐ Check in after making a career move to discuss uncharted territory, develop new skills, and build self-confidence
- ☐ Communicate more effectively with your boss or team
- ☐ Clarify a personal vision or business mission and establish steps toward its fulfillment
- ☐ Talk through a business or work problem that is inhibiting your joy and productivity
- ☐ Think through next stages, face realities, and sort through opportunities
- ☐ Lead others in a more trustworthy and productive manner
- ☐ Explore and answer the question, What will I do when I grow up?
- ☐ Map out your career dreams and step toward them
- ☐ Determine what you want your contribution to be so that you can take back—and give back—your time
- ☐ Redirect your passion and skills after a business buyout, merger, or sale
- ☐ Reconcile your fears and move toward your gifts with energy and enthusiasm